# V. M. Purishkevich

# The Murder of RASPUTIN

Edited & Introduced by MICHAEL E. SHAW
Translated by BELLA COSTELLO

Ardis, Ann Arbor

V. M. Purishkevich, The Murder of Rasputin
Copyright © 1985 by Ardis Publishers
All rights reserved under International and Pan-American Copyright Conventions.
Printed in the United States of America

Translated from the original Russian

Ardis Publishers
2901 Heatherway
Ann Arbor, Michigan 48104


Library of Congress Cataloging in Publication Data
Purishkevich, V. M. (Vladimir Mitrofanovich), 1870-1920.
The murder of Rasputin.
Translation of: Ubiistvo Rasputina.
1. Rasputin, Grigorii Efimovich, 1871-1916—Assassination.
I. Shaw, Michael E. II. Title.
DK254.R3P7913   1984      947.08'3'0924      84-16750
ISBN 0-88233-931-1

# Contents

# List of Illustrations

# INTRODUCTION

Gregory Rasputin, the soothsayer and "holy devil," has, since his appearance in St. Petersburg in 1904, exercised a remarkable attraction on the general public. The story of his powers, the hold he seemed to have exerted on the Tsarina Alexandra and through her on the last Tsar, Nicholas II, continues to fascinate and to repel audiences more than sixty years after his assassination in December 1916. And, while a careful study of either his supposed powers or of the exact nature of his influence at the Russian court remains to be undertaken, Rasputin has already earned a remarkable place in the history of Russia, albeit one that is colored by conjecture, speculation, and hyperbole. He has been credited with the removal of ministers, the sale of offices, the seduction of most of the ladies of the court, bribery, blackmail, deceit, fraud, and treason. The major charge against him was that he was instrumental in the fall of the Romanov dynasty. Many of his contemporaries viewed him as a "sinister" force who, through the Tsarina Alexandra, "the German hussy," deceived the Tsar and betrayed Russia. In the wake of his murder biographers have sought to link his fate to the fate of the Empire, and indeed Rasputin himself is reputed to have maintained that the fate of each was intertwined.

The supposed diary of one of the chief conspirators in the plot to kill Rasputin, published for the first time in English below, is a forceful statement of this interpretation. V. M. Purishkevich, an ultra-rightist member of the State Duma from 1907 and a longtime critic of both constitutionalism and bureaucracy, delivered perhaps the most outspoken public indictment of Rasputin. In a speech to the Duma in November 1916, he described Rasputin as a "sinister force" who, together with Alexandra, was destroying Russia. This diary is, however, more than just a description of the plot and its opera bouffe execution, more than an assessment of a particular, and extreme, variant of Rasputin's influence; it is also a clear statement of the views of the rightists on the nature of the crisis faced by Russia. And, read as such, it is a contribution to our understanding of the autocracy in its last decades, of the mentality of one of its major sources of support, the right, and of the Russian revolution itself.

The interpretation offered by Purishkevich is at first glance fairly simple: the autocracy had become isolated from Russia, and the major cause for this isolation was Rasputin and the control he exerted over the non-Russian Tsarina Alexandra. Remove Alexandra and Rasputin, and the Tsar, restored to contact with and enjoying the support of his subjects, would regain for Russia its natural primacy of place in European affairs and would restore Russia to a condition of tranquility and prosperity. What is implied in this account is, of course, the "natural" state of Russian affairs, the "natural" condition of the Russian subject and his relationship to the "natural" office of the Tsar. But, it is clear that this "natural" condition could only be obtained by dismantling the representative institutions established in 1905-1907, eliminating the hated bureaucratic system which acted as an obstacle between the "people" and the Tsar, and by restoring to the natural elite, the nobility, its proper advisory and administrative role. In order more fully to appreciate the prescriptions offered by Purishkevich in his diary it will be necessary to look at the problems facing the autocracy and Russian society in the little over two decades preceding the revolution. In the survey that follows an assessment of Russia's options, its chances for a successful peaceful resolution of its several crises will be attempted. Further, it will seek to answer the question: Was Rasputin the cause of the autocracy's collapse, or merely, as many have suggested, one of the several symptoms of a system destined for destruction?

When Tsar Nicholas II ascended the throne of the Russian Empire in 1894, many observers both in Russia and abroad regarded his succession as holding out the possibility for major and needed change in the Russian system of government. The autocracy, presided over by Nicholas' father Alexander III since 1881, had shown that it was capable of economic progress, as evidenced by its impressive rate of growth in the 1880s, but there were also signs that these gains had been achieved at the cost of a deteriorating condition in the countryside—both for the nobility and the peasant population. Further, as the famine of 1891 had shown, the autocracy had not improved its capacity for dealing with rural crises; it had neither the apparatus nor, many argued, the will for organizing famine relief. Perhaps more importantly, however, the autocracy, while encouraging the growth of industry, was unprepared for industry's by-product, a growing urban working class population. Labor disputes and connected disorders were treated as simple variants of the traditional rural outburst, and except for some dilatory efforts to correct the worst abuses, were resolved by the same recourse to force. Finally, a growing national consciousness among the subject peoples of the Empire—the unexpected result of the "Russification" policies of the late Tsar—were beginning to present a real threat to the Empire's integrity.

These stresses, on a system already overloaded by the difficulties inherent in administering an empire as farflung and heterogeneous as Russia, had evoked a growing awareness that radical measures had to be undertaken. Nor was this recognition restricted to opponents of autocracy; many of the autocrat's loyal servitors shared the view held by Sergei Witte, then Minister of Commerce, that if Russia were to survive it must transform itself economically and administratively. For these observers, inside the bureaucracy and out, Nicholas' accession to the throne marked a possible turning point for Russia.

Nicholas' personality has been the subject of wide speculation. He has been variously described as an affable, sincere, hard-working man, devoutly religious and a devoted father and husband. He has also been described as weak, suspicious, jealous of advisors whose intelligence seemed superior to his, gullible, vacillatory, stubborn, and vain. There are sufficient evidences for each of these interpretations. One feature of his character which seems to be the most consistently in evidence throughout the twenty-three years of his reign, however, is his unwavering commitment to the maintenance of the autocracy, its powers, its privilege, and its enhanced position in world affairs. In this he was encouraged by his possibly hysterical wife, Alexandra.[1]

What then were the conditions in Russia in 1894? In the countryside the land hungry peasant population, saddled with annual redemption payments and the imposition of indirect taxes to finance the industrial boom, illiterate, superstitious, and chronically backward in technique and organization, lived virtually untouched by the changes in Russia's modernizing urban centers or by the goals of Russian officialdom. While as a whole the peasant community owned more land than it had in 1877, its population too had grown and had resulted in a net decrease in the size of the average holding. Moreover, the uneven increase in ownership had intensified the growing differentiation of this peasant population into wealthy and poor, and had undermined the traditional peasant organization, the commune. The change in the peasantry as a class had also undermined the viability of the myth of the peasantry held by both populist theorists and functionaries of the autocracy.[2] Perhaps the best measure of the peasantry's condition was its growing inability to meet the fiscal demands imposed on it by the autocracy. Despite two reductions in annual redemption payments in the 1880s and two moratoria in the 1890s, the arrears in payment had outstripped the annual assessment by 1900.[3] Clearly, the condition of the peasantry was desperate. And yet, the autocracy's responses oscillated between negligence and repression. While a Peasant Bank had been established in 1881, available funds fell far short of peasant needs, and the possible benefits to be derived from the abolition of the salt and poll taxes in the 1880s would be undercut by the imposition of new indirect taxes (alcohol in 1894), by continued taxation of such items as tobacco, sugar, mineral oil, and matches, and by the tariff and export policies of the government. Study commissions established in both the Ministry of Interior and the Ministry of Finance could only agree that something had to be done to ease the peasant's condition. In general, however, the autocrat and his advisors seemed to regard the peasantry as a resource whose yield should be maximized at a minimum cost to the government. Thus, deteriorating conditions in the countryside were usually resolved by ordinary extraordinary means: troops, police, and in the one monumental effort to legalize arbitrary power, the establishment of land captains (*zemskie nachal'niki*) in 1889.[4] Thus, the unresolved peasant problem and the autocracy's approach to its solution would be an important element in deciding the fate of the latter.

The position of the nobility can be seen as a corollary to the peasant's condition and as a part of the dilemma facing Tsarist Russia. Despite governmental efforts to shore up this class as a whole, or even to "bet on the sober and the strong" by insuring the continued domination of the nobility in provincial affairs, the nobility suffered a continued loss of status in both economic and social-political terms. By 1905 noble ownership of land had fallen by over 25% from its 1878 level; it owned only one-third of the arable land in Russia. Its level of indebtedness, a good indicator of its economic vitality, had risen dramatically, to an estimated level of 50% of all holdings under mortgage. The continued decline of the nobility was not all due to the nobility's frivolity (as presented so vibrantly in Chekhov's plays), or even to its resistance to improved methods and technique. The major challenge facing the noble producer was increased competition—from both foreign and domestic producers. Domestically, the noble producer faced increased competition from a variety of sources. In the Western borderlands, the major challenge came from the more productive Polish nobility, a segment of the peasant community, and from urban middlemen (processors, packagers, and shippers). Elsewhere, the challenges to noble primacy came from similar non-noble spheres. The result in each case was the same: diminishing profits, a diminished share of the total acreage under cultivation, and often bankruptcy.[5] The noble's position was also under attack in both the social and the political spheres. Its preeminence in Russian society was challenged by the new industrial and commercial sectors, by the growing professional classes, and by the bureaucracy. The noble preeminence, given legal definition in the late eighteenth century, had undergone considerable erosion during the nineteenth century. The decline in what had been a noble monopoly can be measured by two seemingly opposite reactions. On the one hand, an increased apathy affected a part of the nobility, generating its self-imposed isolation on its estates, or its escapism into a round of European tours and extravagance, and its absence from organs of popular "representation," i.e., provincial assemblies and the zemstva. This reflected the noble decline as did the aggressive resentment which the nobility directed against segments of the non-noble population. Some of the resentment was directed against Jews, national minorities, the "masses." Some was directed against the bureaucracy—or "plutocracy"—a nameless, faceless horde which surrounded, and in this view, misinformed, the Tsar. In sum, this class was in the midst of a crisis of identity, no longer sure of its own identity and function, no longer convinced of the proper role it should play in Russian society. What is most true of this class as a whole, however, is that it was not able to formulate—in the 1890s, in 1905, in 1917—a viable alternative to its traditional role vis-a-vis the people, vis-a-vis the Tsar.

The 1890s not only marked a change in the political leadership of Russia, but also witnessed what many call a reawakening of society. The thirteen-year reign of Alexander III had been one of unrelenting repression and reaction in which any form of dissent, any vocal criticism of Russian government or society, no matter how timorous, had been effectively muzzled. Alexander III, the successor to the "Tsar liberator," ended all discussion of reform, and especially all possibilities of reform "from below." There were no plans for constitutional reform, for representative assemblies, for popular input into affairs of society or state. Instead, there had been an accelerated growth in centralized, bureaucratic rule, an increased emphasis on uniformity and on control of the disparate elements and groups in the Russian Empire. The result included the effort to integrate (or subordinate) the so-called representative agencies—the zemstva and other local units of self-government—into the centralized apparatus of the state. Similarly, differentiations in the Russian population, within classes, between different ethnic groups—which served to render more difficult their effective administration— were systematically subjected to governmental interference and pressure. Among the keynotes of this era were the Russification program noted above, the growth in the powers of the Ministry of Interior, and the extension of the latter into the lowest levels of society. The effort to simplify, to make uniform, to systematize were a part of the regime's overall strategy of economic growth. And, while this strategy would produce unexpected results in other areas, it had been largely successful in achieving its ends. The rate of growth for the period was one of the highest achieved by any of the great powers.

The limits of this strategy were increasingly apparent in the nineties, however. By mid-decade Russia began to experience its first serious urban disturbances since the era of the Great Reforms in the 1860s. In 1896 a wave of strikes, touched off by work stoppages in the textile industry in St. Petersburg, swept throughout much of the newly industrialized western and southwestern provinces, as well as through the Baltic and Polish provinces. These strikes were followed by the first systematic efforts to organize the new industrial class, then estimated to number in the neighborhood of 2-3 million workers. Although the law of 1874 had made explicitly illegal any workers' organizations which created "ill-feeling" between workers and owners, small groups did begin to organize and to agitate for reform. While strikers' demands were economic (better safety conditions, higher wages, cash payment, and shorter hours), the autocracy's reflexive and brutal response to the strikers—the use of strike breakers and of troops, the arrest of "ringleaders," and the imposition of stiff fines and penalties—made even these demands potentially political in nature.

The autocracy's repressive response to the wave of strikes also rekindled the radical opposition to the regime—effectively shattered during the preceding reign. The mid-to-late nineties saw a resurgence of radicalism and radical activity among both student groups and the more diffuse Russian "intelligentsia." The old populist movement (*Narodnichestvo*) re-emerged in the late nineties as a new, more militant

17

organization dedicated to the overthrow of the autocracy and to the establishment of an agrarian-based socialist society. This revitalized populist movement, however, also sought to minister to the needs of the new urban classes as well, and began to make inroads among the working class groups of provincial Russia (Saratov, Tambov, etc.). The chief spokesman for this new populism, or its chief theoretician, was Viktor Chernov. Chernov, unlike his populist antecedents, accepted as a fact the growing role and the importance of the industrial sector in Russian society, and of the urban working class. But, he argued that the peasant population and peasant institutions still held out the best hope for Russia. Under his leadership, a new party, the Socialist Revolutionary Party (SR) would emerge as one of the chief forces of opposition to the autocracy. While efforts to organize had been frustrated in the 1890s inside Russia, the SR organizers had begun publication of a newspaper for the propagation of their message in 1900 (entitled *Revolutionary Russia*), and in 1902 delegates met in Berlin to establish the SR party formally.

The organization of the SRs was accompanied by a similar development among other groups hostile to autocracy. The first organized Marxist and liberal opposition groups also emerged from the tumult of the late 1890s. As for the former, Russian intellectuals had first been introduced to Marx in the 1870s, and while study groups had been organized in the emigration in the 1880s, the first Marxist organization would be formed only in response to the famine of 1891 and to the growth of urban worker unrest. The early efforts at organization met the same fate as that of the SRs—a national meeting in Minsk in 1898 was torpedoed by the arrest of its leaders. But, in 1900 the representatives of several groups, including the "father" of Russian marxism, George Plekhanov, Julius Martov, and Vladimir Lenin, met in Stuttgart, Germany, where they agreed to publish a central organ—*Iskra* (*The Spark*). This was followed, in 1903, by the "Second" Social Democratic Congress which, while it resulted in a split between Lenin and his followers (the Bolsheviks—Majority) on the one hand, and the Mensheviks (the Minority), including Martov and Plekhanov on the other, nonetheless established Russian Social Democracy as an organized force of opposition to the autocracy. And, like the SRs, the Social Democrats (SD) argued that effective reform could not be achieved within the limits of the autocracy; it could only come after its overthrow.

These groups, SD and SR, the radical opponents of the autocracy, were not the only ones to organize in the late nineties. Russian moderates of a variety of shades also began to organize in this same period. Russian moderates—liberals—can be divided into three general categories: those who sought a radical restructuring of the regime and the introduction of constitutional forms specifically limiting the executive power of the autocrat; those who sought for the "people" some limited representation; and those, the most conservative element, whose goal was the reunion of the autocracy with his subjects. These latter, "Slavophile" liberals, wanted only an advisory role for Russia's classes, and were suspicious of the wholesale importation of Western political institutions into Russia. What all of these groups shared, however, was the sense that some reform had to be enacted if Russia were to be spared the catastrophe of social and political collapse. These groups also shared in a belief that reform could come within the context of the autocracy, and that revolution need not be the only path (indeed, should not be the path) to reform. Between 1896 and 1902 these three currents of liberal thought established formal organizations with which to push for their programs. The slavophile contingent held a national Zemstvo Congress in 1902 (at the home of its chief spokesman, the head of the Moscow Zemstvo Board, Shipov); moderate constitutionalists also adhered to this Zemstvo Union. The more radical liberals—advocates of strict constitutionalism—formed, in 1903, a Union of Liberation in Switzerland. Earlier, they had inaugurated a newspaper, *Osvobozhdenie* (*Liberation*), published in Stuttgart and edited by an ex-marxist, Peter Struve. These three groups would formally emerge in 1905 as the Octobrist and the Constitutional Democratic (KD) parties.

Thus, by the end of the nineteenth century, large segments of educated Russian society had organized for the first time in Russia's history for the expressed purpose of effecting reform. The only group on the political spectrum which had not yet organized formally was the right. This should not be surprising. That they had as yet failed to do so should give some insight into the nature and limitations of the right once, in the wake of the constitutional experiment of 1905, they do begin to make hesitating steps toward the creation of political groupings and parties. The right, naturally enough composed primarily of the nobility, viewed itself in personal relationship to the autocrat. Until 1905 no political party was legal; no political rights existed. Indeed, Russia remained in large part as it had been under Tsar Paul who, in 1800, noted that no one in Russia had any importance beyond that granted him by the Tsar. The duration of this importance, he went on, was similarly determined. And, while the nobility's personal connection to the autocracy had been seriously attenuated, its commitment to this ideal inhibited it from forming political organizations which might have been seen as a challenge to the autocracy. After 1905, when the existence of a representative assembly made such a position untenable, they would nonetheless persist in viewing themselves—even as an organized political group—in terms of this antiquated personal relationship.[6]

In tracing the rise of an organized opposition to the autocracy there is the implicit danger of assuming that one or several of these groups represented or understood the goals or desires of the discontented urban and rural populations, that one or more of them represented a viable and representative alternative to the autocracy. Indeed, more evidence exists for arguing the opposite, that none understood and thus that none could successfully harness this resentment and discontent. Did the SRs, the SDs, the liberals, or even the rightist groups, articulate the views and interests of the constituents they claimed for themselves? Or, did all of these groups engage in combat with the autocracy in isolation from the very groups for which they presumed to speak? While these points are debatable, they are also pivotal to any assessment of the options available to Russia at the turn of the century, and in 1917. That each of the political groups shared vis-a-vis the population an aprioristic vision of what this population needed is clear. Each group or shading had, too, its own image of the future—be it marxist or liberal. What remains to be seen, what is so far only suggested, is whether these separate images of Russia's future left room for, accommodated, the occluded vision of the masses.

The first test of the viability of the autocracy and the strength of the opposition occurred in 1905. The background to 1905, the events that led to what many have called the "dress rehearsal" for 1917, is a complex of social, economic, and political crises. Economically, the country had been in a slump since 1897 and, when poor harvests occurred in 1902, the economic slump was compounded by a rural crisis of ominous proportions. These two developments set off a chain reaction of peasant unrest and urban unemployment, urban disorder and strikes, which continued to build toward the revolution. Perhaps the autocracy could have continued to approach these problems as it had in the past—through a policy of repression—but this time Russia was also involved in a losing war with Japan. The origins of this conflict in Asia need not detain us here, but its importance lies in the strain it placed on the autocracy at a moment of domestic crisis. Having committed itself to an Asian empire, the autocracy had suddenly found itself in a war which not only did not deflect public opinion from domestic concerns (a hope expressed by Minister of Interior von Pleve), but one which exacerbated the domestic crisis and seemed to underscore the need for reform.

Initially the call for reform embraced almost the whole spectrum of Russian politics (with the exception of the right). As early as 1904 liberals had sought to apply pressure on the autocracy by organizing (à la the French example of 1788-1789 and 1848-1849) banquets and meetings. At the same time the radical campaign for the overthrow of the autocracy took a more exigent form when a wave of terrorist attacks, executed by the SR terrorist wing the "Battle Organization," killed a number of governmental officials, including the hapless von Pleve referred to above. The government's response was its traditional one— a promise of unspecified future reform accompanied by a crackdown on the leaders of the opposition. This policy seemed to work, as it always had, until January 1905.

Bloody Sunday is the symbolic beginning of the revolution of 1905, the point at which disparate groups and unconnected crises join together in what appeared to be a united front for change. On January 19, 1905 a peaceful march by over 100,000 workers, their wives and children, all followers of the curious priest, police employee, and union organizer, Father Gapon, was fired on by the police. In the aftermath of this bloody event (in which over 100 were killed), the strike movement, the moderate call for reform, and even the peasant uprisings seemed to galvanize against the autocracy.

As the strike movement mounted and spread throughout the spring of 1905 the government sought to appease the opposition by announcing a new cabinet shuffle and by the promise of systemic reform. The reform, later named after Bulygin, the Minister of Interior whose task it had been to elaborate it, would not be published until August. By this time the tide of opposition had already carried the public beyond the offer of advisory status for the people's representatives.

Throughout the spring and summer, liberal, SR, SD, and peasant organizations flourished. While some of the more moderate elements of the liberal movement (Shipov *et al*) would have been willing to accept the proposals of the Bulygin package, the continued urban and the accelerating rural unrest made such a program unfeasible. For its part, too, the autocracy was carried along by events because, while the army was still in Manchuria, it could not clamp down on the whole of Russian society. Those troops in European Russia not engaged in the war were considered too unreliable to use against the population; a consideration made all the more germane when the crew of the battleship Potemkin mutinied against its officers, bombarded Odessa "in support" of an ongoing strike there, and then set sail for safe harbor in Jassy on the Romanian coast. Thus, with society united in opposition to "staying the course" and with the autocracy unable to bring sufficient force to bear against it and hovering on the brink of bankruptcy, the revolution appeared to be on the verge of success.

The autocracy's position became even more untenable in September when the wave of rural risings continued its upward spiral and when a general strike movement paralyzed the two capitals of Moscow and St. Petersburg. In the heat of the crisis, Tsar Nicholas summoned his former Minister of Commerce back to office and appealed to him to chart a course for the autocracy. Count Sergei Witte's advice to the Tsar is well known. Outlining to Nicholas his options, he told the Tsar that he had two choices: to appoint (as had been done in 1877 at the height of People's Will campaign against the autocracy) a supreme military commander with absolute powers to suppress all elements of the opposition, or to give in to the opposition and grant a constitution. Nicholas' choice was the publication of the October Manifesto.

The October Manifesto has been the subject of much analysis and debate. The major points of contention are, what did the Tsar promise, and why did he promise it? In general, historians find inconsistencies between the Manifesto and the decrees and rescripts which followed it over the course of the six months following its publication. A key to an understanding of the Tsar's intention and purpose can be found in the opening lines of the Manifesto: "We, Tsar by the grace of God..." In his own mind the Tsar was giving a gift to his subjects, not responding to pressure, not bowing to the demands for constitutional reform, nor recognizing the legitimacy of these demands, but granting a boon to those entrusted into his care by divine mandate.

The October Manifesto promised the establishment of a representative legislative body, the rule of law, and a guarantee of broad civil liberties. Its impact was immediate. Liberals of all shadings either embraced the document as the touchstone for Russia's future (the Octobrists), or, as was true of the more radical wing, the Constitutional Democrats (KD), viewed it as a beginning, a context within which to push for further reform. This effectively shattered the illusion of a united opposition. Nothing could have indicated this more clearly than the fate of the new general strike called in November. Liberal leaders denounced this worker-led strike. Industrialists who earlier in the summer had encouraged workers to demonstrate—to increase pressure on the autocracy—called for its suppression. The ever-present suspicion of the working class—the people (*liudi*)—was brought to the surface not simply because of the October Manifesto, but because the strike's leadership, constituted into a workers' council (Soviet), also called for the overthrow of the autocracy by force. This maximalist socialist program frightened even those moderates still to be satisfied by the Tsar's promises for reform.

The autocracy, more sure of itself, more solvent in the wake of loans secured by Witte, and possessed of reliable troops returned from Manchuria after the conclusion of the Portsmouth Peace with Japan, reverted to its practice of repression. The general strike was broken, the strike's leaders (including Leon Trotsky) were arrested and imprisoned. By late November, early December, the autocracy had regained substantial control over the urban population. Suppression of the rural uprisings would begin in earnest later in 1906.

To complement this revanche of autocratic authority, the Tsar issued a series of decrees whose purpose was to give definition to the promises made in October. These separate decrees, issued between December and April, 1906, and called collectively "The Fundamental Laws," fell far short of the constitutional changes anticipated by all groups left of the moderate or Slavophile liberals. Instead of the unicameral legislature promised in October, the Tsar announced the creation of two chambers: the State Council, or upper house, half of whose members were appointed by the Tsar, the other half elected by the nobility; and the State Duma, a popularly elected body, but one whose constituency was restricted by decree. Even moderates were dismayed by the veto power the upper chamber was to have over the Duma. Similarly, the demand for a Cabinet of Ministers responsible to the Duma went unheeded; the Tsar would appoint (and remove) ministers at will. Perhaps the most ominous feature of the Fundamental Laws was Article 87. This article gave the Tsar or his ministers the right to issue decrees having the force of law in the absence of a sitting Duma. The only stipulation was that such decrees had to obtain the approval of the Duma in its next meeting. Article 87 would become the major legislative instrument of the autocracy in the subsequent "constitutional era."

Despite these restrictions, elections to the First State Duma drew the enthusiastic involvement of the voting public; even the SRs and the SDs reluctantly decided to participate. The campaign was an excited one which even the intervention of the police in favor of rightist candidates did not dampen. When the votes were tallied, they represented a dramatic victory for the parties which called for the extension of constitutional guarantees. The first Duma was dominated by the Kadet (KD) party which persisted in its demand for universal suffrage, ministerial accountability, and the elimination of the State Council. The result: deadlock. The first Duma, named the Duma of Popular Hope, lasted a mere seventy-two days before the Tsar, utilizing his right to prorogue this representative body, closed it and called for new elections.

The campaign for the second Duma, the Duma of National Frustration, was a bitter one, and illustrated the growing disillusionment of the population. The Kadets, who had reacted to the Duma's preemptory closing by issuing the Vyborg Manifesto, were a special target of police harassment. Any of its members who had signed this manifesto—calling on the population to oppose the government's "illegal" prorogation by disobeying any decree not approved by the Duma—were barred from standing for office.

Campaign meetings for the Kadets and for other leftist parties (SD and SR) were systematically disrupted, campaign literature was seized, and voters were intimidated by the police against supporting "radical" candidates. Despite this campaign of harassment, the Second State Duma, elected in February, 1907, was more radical and intransigent in its opposition to the autocracy than had been its predecessor. It was also even more short-lived.

The Second State Duma was prorogued on June 3, 1907. Nicholas II closed this Duma because the deadlock between this body and the autocracy was unresolvable. The Second Duma was dominated by the socialists who, with the support of peasant delegates, were able effectively to prevent any substantive action. Instead, the Tsar and his ministers were subjected to unrelenting criticism, and were treated to the call for the autocracy's overthrow. In addition to continuing the Kadet call for universal suffrage, ministerial responsibility, and land reform, this Duma also rejected the Stolypin Land Program (named after the new Minister of Interior who originated it) which had been enacted under the infamous Article 87.

In the wake of the dismissal of the Second Duma, Stolypin introduced a series of reforms which constituted an administrative coup d'état. A new electoral law was issued which deprived students, soldiers, sailors, workers, landless peasants, and the minorities of any effective representation. The result was the election of what was popularly termed the "Masters' Duma," one dominated by the Great Russian landowning and industrialist classes. While called the Masters' Duma by the public, this body's majority was so timorous in its dealings with the Tsar and his ministers that it survived its full five-year term.

The five years of the Third Duma and the first several years of its successor, the Fourth Duma, are generally described as the years of constitutional experimentation in Russia. It is to this period that historians look when attempting to assess the possibilities for peaceful change. And, while this period has been the subject of protracted and continuing debate, it is to it that we need now to direct our attention.

The period 1907-1914 has been presented as the litmus test for the autocracy. Many commentators have sought to demonstrate the autocracy's resilience in this period, politically, and the great strides it made socially and economically, and have concluded from this demonstration that its chances for survival had been much enhanced. Others have argued that the stresses which had threatened the autocracy with dissolution before 1905 had not only not been removed, but had been increased by the "positive" economic and social change.

In the political sphere, the nature of political life in Russia had been profoundly altered by the publication of the October Manifesto and the Fundamental Laws. And, even while subsequent action, including the restriction of the franchise, had limited the effect of these earlier decrees, technically the Tsar's unlimited power had, by gaining definition, been limited. How great these limitations were, what hope they offered for the development toward truly representative government on the western model form the basis for a continuing debate.

Those who view the era with optimism point to several specific areas to support their argument of positive change: domination of the Duma by moderate parties; cooperation of the government with the Duma to enact important social legislation; the extension of the Duma's purview; and in general, the Duma's integration into the governmental structure. On the first issue, one can point to the strength of the Octobrist Party during much of the Third Duma. This party, the most moderate sector of the liberal movement, explicitly accepted the terms of the October Manifesto (and the Fundamental Laws) as the framework for the Russian state. Unlike the Kadets in 1905-1907, they did not seek confrontation with the autocracy, but rather sought to demonstrate their reliability to the Tsar and his advisors. Their governing principle was the belief that such a demonstration would eventuate in the extension of greater responsibility, greater power to the Duma. On the surface, this strategy seems to have been correct. Throughout the first years of the Third Duma, the policy of cooperation animated both the government and the Duma. The President of the Council of Ministers, Peter Stolypin, pursued an active policy of cooperation.[7] The result of this cooperation was a set of moderate reforms, including the agrarian reform, the institution of compulsory, universal, and free primary education, the extension of the zemstvo to nine additional western provinces, and (in 1912) the enactment of a workers' insurance plan. All of these point to the acceptance of the Duma as partner in the affairs of state. Similarly, Duma committees are credited with having had considerable influence on the elaboration of the reform programs for both the army and navy. And, in this period, the Duma did obtain control over a larger portion of the budget, from 53% to 62% of the

total. Thus, those who view this period with some
equanimity argue that moderate parties had succeeded
in bridging the gap with the autocracy and in so
doing had taken great strides toward healing the rift
in Russian society.

These analysts are answered by others who
point to the limited nature of these changes and to
the weakness of the moderate control of the Duma.
They begin their analysis by pointing to the inherent
flaws in the Duma itself, its restrictions. First, they
argue that the Duma, popularly viewed as the
"Masters'," could do little to heal the rift between
the people and the autocracy. Indeed, the revised
franchise virtually excluded the urban and rural poor
as well as the national minorities, while assuring the
near monopoly of the landowning and industrialist
classes. At best, only a small section had been
admitted into the corridors of power. As for the
question of moderate dominance, these critics point
to the Octobrists' inability to obtain a majority in
either the Third or Fourth Dumas, the growing
strength of the Nationalist Party after 1909, and to
the virtual collapse of moderate parties by 1914. The
experiment in cooperation with the autocracy had
succeeded in making these moderates less, not more,
acceptable to the broad population.

As for the efficacy of cooperation with the
government, this too is defined as a failure. Noting
that the two most important pieces of legislation
enacted in this period, the extension of the zemstvo,
and the agrarian reform bill, were enacted under
Article 87 these critics argue that little had been
accomplished to alter the autocracy or its methods.

What is most telling in this critique of moderate
achievements, however, is the contention that the

spirit of cooperation was itself restricted to the Octobrists and to Stolypin, and did not extend to include others of the Tsar's ministers, the Tsar himself, or other political parties. Indeed, this policy of cooperation was only successful as long as Stolypin headed the Council of Ministers, as long as he, and not the Octobrists, planned the agenda of cooperation, and thus was severely limited even in the best of times. After 1909 these limitations became more and more apparent as Stolypin sought the support not of the Octobrists but of the new Nationalist Party. The policy of cooperation lost all credence after Stolypin's assassination in 1911 and his replacement by Kokovtsov. In the years following, the ministers sought not further cooperation with the Duma, but rather its emasculation.[8] In 1912 and again in 1914, the Council of Ministers debated the issue of a restructuring of the Duma, and its restriction to strictly advisory capacity. That this was twice seriously considered indicates the depth of the autocracy's commitment to the Duma.

The crux of the foregoing argument is over the question of the Tsar's acceptance of the idea of sharing power with the Duma, or with any other group or individual. There is little evidence to suggest that Nicholas had changed his basic conceptualization of his role. He was an absolute monarch who believed it his duty to rule in God's name. In this he was supported by Alexandra, who constantly urged upon him a policy of firmness, and whose hatred of the Duma and of representative institutions is well known. More than being a result of Nicholas' personality, however, the issue is whether autocracy and system, autocracy and the rule of law, are in any sense harmonizable or compatible. Nicholas did not oppose the Duma simply because he was petty and jealous, but because he was an autocrat. In his view, the office of the autocrat was a great trust which had to be defended and preserved. His removal of ministers at will is another example of this. Much is made of the increased rationality of government in Russia in the late nineteenth and early twentieth centuries, of the increased rule of law, of system. The flaw in all of this is, of course, that the Tsar was external to the system, that he could, like the medieval God, intervene anywhere in the system, to punish or to reward. The result was inevitable. Rather than the formal institutionalization of power, personal connection, personal relation to the Tsar remained the criterion for position and the exercise of power. Hence, ministers did not simply exercise a set amount of influence or power, nor was this influence necessarily limited to their individual ministries. They could, if their connection to the Tsar was close, have the deciding voice over issues properly the province of their colleagues in the Council of Ministries. That both their appointment or removal, and the determination of the extent of their power, remained a matter of the Tsar's whim, did not make for the development of stable cabinet politics. Ministers, by virtue of their dependence on the autocrat, intrigued against each other, and competed for the favor of the Tsar.

This problem of ministerial instability and intrigue was only slightly improved during Stolypin's tenure as both Minister of Interior and President of the Council of Ministers (1907-1911). His control of the Interior Ministry, his energy, and the support of the Tsar, allowed him to dominate the Council of Ministers (and, some have suggested, the Tsar).

33

After Stolypin's assassination, Nicholas was careful to avoid the concentration of this much power in one minister's hands—fearful, perhaps of being eclipsed by a subordinate—and given the evidence seemed to delight in filling the Council with wildly disparate political figures ranging from arch-reactionaries like A. Makarov and N. Maklakov to more progressive ministers like A. Krivoshein. Thus, ministerial vulnerability, ministerial intrigue were encouraged.

In the economic sphere, two related issues are generally debated: did Russia experience "self-sustaining" growth and did this growth have a stabilizing or de-stabilizing effect on Imperial Russian society?

The leading proponent of the argument that Russia experienced a healthy growth pattern is the economic historian Alexander Gerschenkron.[9] He argues that Russia's economic development had not only been substantial, but that it had become self-sustaining (irreversible); the most important feature of this economic development was the growth of Russian investment capital. Russia did go through another boom period following the dislocation of 1902-1905. The figures for overall industrial growth for the period are impressive—a six per cent annual rate of growth for the period 1906-1914, nine per cent for 1909-1914. Moreover, for the whole period (1880-1914), Russia had scored impressive gains in heavy industry: it had increased iron production by 1,000 per cent, and in steel production it had become the world's fourth largest producer. Similarly, railroad construction and metallurgical industries had sustained enormous increases. Even in exports, a 50% increase after 1905 could be pointed to to indicate the robust nature of the Russian economy.

Critics of this picture of economic health do not quarrel with these figures, but argue that they do not give the full picture. To begin, the figures do not show that Russia had emerged as an independent industrial nation. And, while the rate of growth was impressive, it was as much the result of external factors as it was of the growth of native investment or native initiative. To underscore this point, critics point out that foreign investment continued to play a large role in the development of Russian industry. In 1916 foreign investment was estimated at 2,243 billion rubles (the largest investor was France, followed by Britain, Germany, and Belgium). This capital investment was concentrated in those industries whose rate of growth had been the highest. Foreigners owned one-third of all the stock of Russia's joint stock companies (50% in metallurgy and mining, 67% in the new electrical industry). Similarly, the growth of Russia's railroads is attributed to heavy state investment. Two-thirds of the railroad lines in Russia were state-owned. By 1916 Russia had also accumulated the largest foreign debt in the world (5.4 billion rubles), and while part of this figure could be attributed to Russia's involvement in the war, the overall picture is not one of a healthy, self-generating economy.[10] Nor, the critics argue, was it independent of its major investors—France and Britain.

On the basis of these evidences, these critics conclude that Russian industry continued to be dominated by foreign investment and state control. The former is especially important because it made Russia more vulnerable to its major creditors, more susceptible to their political influences, and ultimately led her into a conflict from which the autocracy did not emerge—World War I.

These critics argue that the more important consideration in this assessment of Russia's economic development was its impact on the social and political spheres. The point here is that the economic advances made by Russia in this period exacerbated the social and political conflicts in Russian society and had a destabilizing impact on the autocracy. The major spokesman for this view is Leopold Haimson. Haimson argues that this period witnessed a dual polarization of Russian society: between the government and educated (privileged) society and between the latter and the broader Russian population.[11] There is ample evidence to suggest such a split even before 1914, the splits are compounded once Russia finds itself in a losing war.

By the end of 1907 the workers' disturbances had been forcibly suppressed, not to revive again until after 1910. In roughly this same period the workers did achieve at least one notable success, the insurance coverage noted above. And, while strikes were still illegal, they had won some wage and hour benefits. The dual question is, however, did the autocracy alter its attitude or policies toward the working class, and did the worker develop a new loyalty to the regime absent in 1905? Soviet scholars are united in arguing that the workers developed a greater consciousness of their class and interests in this period and therefore increased their hostility to the autocracy and the capitalist classes and institutions. While this is overdrawn, Haimson has argued that the workers did develop, if not a "proletarian consciousness," a sense of their identity separate from, even hostile to, the privileged classes and the autocracy.

Moreover, they adopted an independent stance economically and socially which rejected all forms of moderate leadership—even up to and including the leadership of Menshevik union leaders. Haimson's most provocative point, however, is his contention that the workers, especially those in the most advanced geographic and industrial sectors (the metallurgical workers and notably those in the Petersburg guberniia) repeatedly focused on important new grievances which demonstrated their sense of identity as workers and their alienation from other groups in urban society: on questions of dignity and respect. This is an especially telling development because neither the autocracy nor the industrialist class had managed to rid itself of the image of the worker as a displaced peasant and thus had continued to treat the worker in a traditional, patriarchal, patronizing manner. This opposition of images of the worker was as potentially explosive as any economic grievance—as the increasingly political nature and staccato incidence of strikes in 1910-1914 indicate.

Between 1910-1914 the wave of strikes mounted both quantitatively and qualitatively. Whereas there had been close to three million workers on strike in 1905, and only 1.3 million on strike in the first six months of 1914, these figures are more dramatic than they appear to be. Haimson notes that almost 75% of the strikes in 1914 are political in nature. Moreover, their success rate is much lower than in either 1905 or 1906—a sign not so much of the autocracy's greater efficiency in strike management in 1914 as it is of the greater frustration and unrelenting worker opposition to the status quo.

The condition of the rural population is also one on which historians are divided. Did the peasantry's condition improve after 1905? Were the bases for its integration into the modernizing urban society being laid in this period? Was there any hope that this class could form a cohesive and stable bulwark for the autocracy? Numerous commentators have noted that the autocracy's policies toward the peasantry were informed by its concern for rapid industrialization, that the peasantry both before and after 1905 had been designated as the group which would bear the major burden for this economic modernization, and that its condition, the question of its improvement, was of secondary importance. The peasantry remained a resource to be plumbed. It also remained a problem: how to control it, how to harness it, how to prevent it from disrupting the economic progress planned for Russia? The autocracy's answer to this question was provided by the Stolypin reform of 1906. This reform, which Stolypin described as a "wager on the sober and the strong," was designed to create an independent peasant class, in the French style and for the same reasons; the French peasantry had been a pillar of conservatism since 1800. The Stolypin reform allowed for the dissolution of the commune and the consolidation of individual holdings into privately owned plots. The belief was that the new class of peasant holders would act as a moderating agent against chronic peasant unrest. It is a remarkable piece of legislation in that it effectively reversed the autocracy's position on the commune inaugurated in 1861. With this decree in 1906, complemented by subsequent decrees in 1910 and 1911, the peasant could freely leave the commune and establish his own compact holding. The assessments of the results of this reform are mixed. Soviet scholars argue that it benefited only the wealthy peasant and the average peasant was left untouched by it. Many western historians have sought to show that with time this reform would have had the desired effect. Critics of this view stress that by 1915 less than 10% of the peasants who had left the commune had consolidated their holdings. That is, peasants continued, for the most part, to cultivate in the same fashion as on the eve of the reform. The result: no improvement in the peasant's standard of living, no increase in output, and consequently, no substantial development toward the creation of a "sober" and conservative peasant middle class.

To return briefly to the privileged classes, the record seems to indicate not greater stability but greater disillusionment and greater isolation from the autocracy on the one hand and from the lower classes on the other. The story is not necessarily an exclusively Russian one. At the same time in England, in France, Germany, and the Austro-Hungarian Empire, the precepts and presumptions of the "moderate" or the "liberal" constituency were in the process of being shattered—on the shoals of Labor in England, syndicalism and socialism in France, and socialism, nationalism, racism and a variety of radical popular movements in both Germany and the Austro-Hungarian Empire. In Russia, as well, the groups which would normally have constituted the base for moderate politics had not only to challenge the unlimited authority of the autocracy but were themselves challenged by nationalist movements, peasant parties, and socialists. The result was not simply that the moderate parties that represented privileged society were less self-assured, but that they were increasingly divided over the proper course to adopt. Their history is a sad one. The failure of the policy of cooperation with the autocracy was the major cause for the defection of industrialist supporters and the creation of the Progressist party in 1912. In 1913 the Octobrists were further weakened by the open split between urban and rural wings, once more, over the issue of the party's proper relationship to the autocracy. These defections and splits, when added to the continued Kadet-Octobrist hostility, permanently rendered illusory any hope that a united moderate opposition could be formed to push the autocracy into reform. Tragically, the moderates could put forward no alternative to cooperation with the autocracy. Their fear of "revolution" from below on the one hand, their presumption that they were the proper spokesmen for the population (the heirs apparent to the autocracy) on the other, prevented them from launching a sustained drive to win support outside the urban centers or beyond the realm of the professional classes. The bankruptcy of these parties was already evident in 1914. The Kadets had only nine provincial offices in all of Russia and their membership had dropped from a high of 100,000 in 1907 to 24,000 in 1914. The Octobrist split had all but paralyzed this party, and the Progressists were too narrowly constituted to offer real leadership to the moderates.

Nor was the picture of disarray and disunity confined to the moderate parties. Even the Nationalist party had suffered from its contact with the autocracy. By 1914 this party too was disillusioned, divided, and dispirited. Its decline, as with the moderates, can be traced to its pursuit of a policy of collaboration with an autocracy which by its nature spurned all political collaboration.

By 1914 all political parties were on the verge of political bankruptcy; the war would produce no additional credit. Whether or not the war accelerated the drift toward the breakdown of the autocracy is a much debated issue. What is clear is that the crisis produced by Russia's entry into the war exacerbated the tensions already present in the Russian body politic. Moreover, the defeats removed from the autocracy its last source of support—the army. During the course of the war it became clear that the system presided over by the Tsar was incapable of managing the Russian empire.

The war was an unmitigated disaster for Russia. While the initial response to the war—at least in urban centers—had been an outburst of patriotic fervor, the early defeats, the civil and military mismanagement, the chronic shortages, and spiralling inflation, rather quickly transformed this fervor into disenchantment with the regime, a disenchantment so pervasive that it would finally lead to the collapse of the autocracy. What is remarkable about the eventual collapse is that it would not be called or led by any of the leaders of the organized opposition— moderate, liberal, or left.

The sheer number of blunders, the reverses, committed and suffered by the autocracy have all been chronicled elsewhere. For our purposes it will suffice merely to examine the chief political blunders. Primary among these was Nicholas' decision to assume personal command of the Russian armies. Whether his staying in St. Petersburg (renamed the less Germanic Petrograd) would have eased the growing crisis is unlikely, but at the time both supporters and critics regarded his departure for the front as a grave error; henceforth defeats could not be blamed on incompetent generals alone; henceforth the Tsar would be isolated from events in his own capital. This last point has received considerable attention because the vacuum of power created by his departure for the front was rather quickly filled by Alexandra, acting in his name, becoming the filter through which much of his information was passed.

While many writers have yielded to the temptation to blame Alexandra for Russia's final agonies, and while it is quite true that the Tsar did come to rely on her judgment in political matters as well (though by no means did he always accept her counsels), to blame Alexandra is to imply that without her, or with Nicholas in Petrograd, the result would have been quite different. The evidence for such a view is not convincing; rather the opposite is true. The demoralization of all political parties outlined above was not reversed but deepened by the war. It should also be added that the radical parties fared no better during the war. Bolshevik deputies were arrested in December 1914, and most socialist and Socialist Revolutionary publications were closed by the censor. If official harassment were not enough, the initially patriotic response of the working class population added to the demoralized mood of the radical parties. Nor had Nicholas' position on representative institutions undergone a metamorphosis. Nicholas wanted only a docile nonoppositional Duma, and while he was willing to have it function when it presented no threat to the principle of autocracy, he remained unwilling even to contemplate a real sharing of power with it. In effect, the war gave the autocracy the pretext for effecting what it had earlier considered: ". . . the excuse to effect a constitutional coup, to reduce the Fourth Duma in practice from a legislative to a consultative assembly."[12] During the war the Duma was only called when it was convenient to the government, its right to legislate was fundamentally weakened as the Tsar and his ministers resorted to Article 87 as a matter of course. And, even its nonlegislative powers were subjected to official attack, as evidenced by the violation of parliamentary immunity in the arrest and imprisonment of Bolshevik deputies. Instead of a policy of cooperation, the autocracy preferred to ignore the Duma when it was possible, and to use it for its own purposes when it was not.

The effect on the already demoralized parties was as disastrous as it was predictable. The Octobrists, already split in 1913, declined further as many of its members sought more fruitful occupation in extra-Duma war activities. The Kadets chafed under Miliukov's leadership of restraint, and by 1916 had split into at least three discernible factions. The Progressists were similarly in disarray, and even the Nationalists were divided over the party's proper relationship to the heedless autocracy. The Duma's initial policy of restraint, employed for the first year of the war, was replaced in September 1915 by the Progressive Bloc. But, when the Bloc also proved incapable of adopting a more aggressive policy, it lost not only Duma support, but the support of the public. This public—the privileged society which it represented—regarded the Duma as too timid, too insistent on a policy of non-confrontation with the autocracy during the war. On its side, the Duma leadership, as was its tradition, viewed the public (even the urban, privileged sector) as too reckless, and was unwilling to cooperate with it or to subject itself to its demand for a more energetic policy.[13]

Thus, the war broadened the gulf between the Duma and the public, at a moment when its always tenuous connection with the autocracy had been severed by the Tsar and his ministers.

This is the context in which the Rightist deputy Purishkevich hatched his appallingly silly plot to save Russia. To Purishkevich, the solution to Russia's problems was a surgical one—remove the alien growth, Rasputin, and the body politic would again become well. Purishkevich, while himself a buffoon whose career was both suspect and comically sordid, did at least share this view with a large section of the right, and a part of the more conservative Octobrists. Purishkevich, and his co-conspirators, believed that the autocracy was a viable institution, suited to Russia—both because of custom and backwardness —that a "good" Tsar was the best defense against revolution in either its urban or rural guise, and that a Tsar who also heeded the advice of his subjects, the noble class, would insure a prosperous and powerful Russia. Given this general belief, it is not surprising that Rasputin should have become the focus, together with the Tsarina Alexandra, for Purishkevich's critique of Russia. This was, anyway, a safer target than the Tsar himself (it is useful to note that Miliukov's choice of targets was the same in his celebrated "treason" speech to the Duma in the summer of 1916). Safer because neither Rasputin nor Alexandra could claim any popularity in Russian society, safer because it required no deeper analysis of the problems facing Russia.

Rasputin had managed to raise eyebrows and the occasional outcry since his arrival in St. Petersburg in 1904. A barely literate, self-proclaimed holy man, he had at first won considerable support from influential churchmen and society people, and had been introduced to the Tsar and Tsarina in 1905. His hold on the Imperial couple—and especially the Tsarina—has been the subject of a number of speculative and naive works.[14]

Rasputin was only one in a long string of holy men and shamans to have gained access to the royal household. His attraction was not only his claim to great piety—the Tsarina, a convert to Orthodoxy, was an hysterically religious woman—but his ability to calm the hemophilic heir to the Russian throne. Rasputin, according to any number of witnesses, was able to stop the Tsarevich's bleeding with soothing words, and on at least one occasion, with a telegram sent to Tsarskoe Selo (the Imperial residence). The result was that Alexandra became his protectress, overlooking or disbelieving the myriad reports on Rasputin's other, less pious activities.

The reports, assembled by the Ministry of Interior, provide a picture of Rasputin quite unlike that of a simple, pure, and pious peasant. Rasputin, whose form of Christianity can best be described as "salvation through sin"—that is, sin until fatigue overwhelms you and at that point, you attain union with Christ—indulged his remarkable capacity for sin in an endless round of drinking parties, public orgies, and private seductions. These peccadilloes finally cost him the support of many church leaders, but were not conclusive enough for Alexandra who regarded reports of his misdeeds as simple slanders. Rasputin was able to survive several major campaigns to unmask him, and despite being twice ordered by the Tsar to leave the capital, was able to return to St. Petersburg for the final time in 1914. From then until his assassination in December 1916, Rasputin became Alexandra's chief advisor and indeed, in her eyes, the "salvation" of the Russian dynasty.[15] And, it is during this period too that Rasputin's influence and his activities received broader and less indulgent attention. Rasputin was reputed to have been implicated in numerous kick-back schemes, involved in widescale corruption involving banks, munitions and supply firms for the army, but most important was reputed to have enormous political influence because of his friendship with Alexandra. Thus, he is supposed to have been responsible for the dismissal of the Head of the Council of Ministers, Goremykin, the appointment of Sturmer, of Khvostov, Protopopov, and other reactionary and incompetent ministers. To many, his influence seemed to be pervasive and his apartment became the site of daily pilgrimages of both the important and the inconsequential united only by their hope that Rasputin would intercede for them with an appropriate minister, or Alexandra herself. It was perhaps inevitable that this huckster would also have been identified as the "sinister" force responsible for each of the autocracy's failures. Indeed, even Rasputin understood this; and this is probably the best way to interpret his "prophecy" that the autocracy would not long survive him. His growing concern for his safety was translated into protective measures; he was guarded by three separate police agencies by the summer of 1916. Despite this precaution, Rasputin was nonetheless the hapless victim of an assassination plot carried out by one grandduke, a prince, Duma deputy Purishkevich, his wife, and his medical aide, Dr. Lazovert. That this plot was successful should give some proper context both to the efficacy of Rasputin's protection and to the solidity of his powers.

Vladimir Mitrofanovich Purishkevich, the author of the "Diary" published below, was, to be kind, a curious and basically unsound representative of the reactionary right in Russia.[16] There is little published about him in either Soviet or Western literature. Although his name is usually cited in most works on the period—as a representative of rightist obstructionism in the Duma period, as the assassin of Rasputin—nothing beyond short biographic notes or essays exists. One of the most interesting of the latter is an essay titled "Russkii fashist," published in 1925 in Leningrad. The author's use of the then still novel "fascist" gives some clue to the essay's tenor: Purishkevich is characterized as having been a bully, a loud-mouth, and a buffoon—precisely the terms employed to describe Mussolini—and his antics are attributed to no deep-felt beliefs. He was merely an atavism of the old order.[17]

Purishkevich came from a wealthy landowning family in Bessarabia. His family's origins were apparently Moldavian, but the family had attained noble status some three generations before his birth. His grandfather had been an archpriest in the Moldavian church, and his father had served as president of the Akkerman district committee. Purishkevich himself entered public life between 1902 and 1904 as a member of a special commission in the Ministry of Interior (working under von Pleve). He was elected to the Second Duma, but it was not until the Third and Fourth Dumas that he was able to develop fully his particular political style. Whenever possible, Purishkevich sought to disrupt the Duma proceedings, to abuse opponents in the moderate and left parties, and even to hurl insults at the Duma's president. Nor did he restrict himself to verbal attacks; he would also show his disdain for this "representative" body by making faces, twitching, fidgeting, and on at least one occasion by appearing in the Duma sporting a carnation in his fly. His obstructionist behavior got him temporarily expelled from the Duma on several occasions, but even this did not succeed in moderating his approach to politics. And for good reason. Purishkevich was not just acting the fool. He had, like most of the right, joined the Duma not because he respected and supported it, but because the Tsar had been forced to establish it; it was his duty to limit its pernicious influence. Purishkevich regarded the Duma as an alien and harmful importation from the West; moreover, it was, in his view, dominated by dangerous liberal elements who sought the destruction of Russian institutions. Thus, his purpose was not to represent society, but to champion the autocracy. On every issue he supported the preservation of autocracy and the limitation of popular rights—whether it was on the question of Duma rights, or the suspension of the Finnish constitution, Purishkevich consistently upheld the principle of autocracy and the supremacy of Great Russian institutions and culture.

In addition to his role in the Duma, Purishkevich was also reputed to have been an active member in a variety of ultra-reactionary groups—including the Russian Union and the Union of the Archangel Michael—which engaged in anti-Semitic and anti-leftist campaigns. Indeed, it has been suggested that Purishkevich was a major conduit for monies distributed to the Black Hundreds to finance pogroms against the Jewish population. He is also credited with having founded a network of ultraright student groups whose dual purpose was to promote patriotism and to disrupt revolutionary students groups. The nature and extent of these activities has not been documented.[18]

However extensive his non-Duma activities were, Purishkevich seems to have dedicated himself to Russian military victory once war was declared. From that moment on, he spent little time in the Duma, and when there adopted a more sober and serious attitude. Instead, his time and energies were expended on the war effort. Primarily engaged on the Rumanian and Southern fronts, he was involved in obtaining medical and other supplies for the army. The new seriousness of purpose was borne of his conviction that Russia's survival as a culture depended on Russia's victory in the war. This belief naturally made him view with horror the blunders and reverses of the Russian army and civil administration, and led him to search for the cause of these errors. Given his unqualified support of autocracy, he could never bring himself to question the viability of this institution, but he could safely find corruptions in its proper functioning. These corruptions turned out to be poor advisors, time-servers, the plutocracy, but most of all, Rasputin. The result, for Purishkevich as it had been for all conservative spokesmen since Karamzin, was that since the Tsar was surrounded by poor advisors, the autocracy and Russia could only be saved if these were replaced by "true" Russian representatives. This simple equation led Purishkevich into a plot to remove the source of Russia's bad advice: Rasputin. That two of his co-conspirators were of princely families only underscored for him the sanctity of the enterprise, and the urgency of its undertaking.[19] That Rasputin's elimination did not avert the Russian Revolutions of 1917 can be taken as history's judgment of Purishkevich's analysis of Russia's crisis.

### Notes

1. Sir Bernard Pares, in commenting on Nicholas, stresses that his obstinate resistance to reform was the result of his frustrated desire to please his father; as well as his wife's stridency. Bernard Pares, *The Fall of the Russian Monarchy* (New York, 1939), p. 47.
2. On the official myth see Yaney, *The Systematization of Russian Government*. See especially p. 392 and *passim*.
3. G. T. Robinson, *Rural Russia Under the Old Regime* (New York, 1932), pp. 85-86. Arrears equalled an average of 119% for the period 1896-1900.
4. Yaney sees the autocracy's inability to resolve the rural crisis as the result of its self-imposed dilemma: its effort to impose a self-sustaining system in the countryside. The point he omits is, to what purpose? To make society better? To enhance the strength of the autocracy at home and abroad? See p. 365 and passim.
5. See R. Edelman, *Gentry Politics on the Eve of the Russian Revolution* (New Brunswick, N.J., 1980).
6. See, for example, R. Edelman, *Gentry Politics on the Eve of the Russian Revolution*.
7. Whether or not this was a new approach, or simply a renewal of the autocracy's pattern of promises mixed with repression is called into question by Stolypin's corollary program of suppression of all radical parties, unions, and peasant disturbances, including the use of courts martial to try and dispatch radical opponents of the regime.
8. Even before 1911, ministerial cooperation with the Duma was often grudging. For example, the Duma's right to interpellate ministers—compel them to give written responses to formal questions—was generally ignored, or their responses came not within the one month provided by law, but after six or ten or nineteen months.
9. A. Gerschenkron, "Agrarian Politics and Industrialization in Russia, 1861-1917," *Cambridge Economic History*, volume 6, part 2, chapter 8.
10. These critics also point out that while exports had indeed increased by 50% between 1905-1914, less than 5% of these exports were in manufactured goods, more than 50% were in foodstuffs, 33% were from the state-owned timber industry. Thus, Russia remained, in international trade, an agrarian economy.

11. L. Haimson, "The Problem of Social Stability in Urban Russia, 1905-1917," *Slavic Review*, XXIII (December 1964), pp. 619-642, and XXIV (March 1965), pp. 1-22.
12. R. Pearson, *The Russian Moderates and the Crisis of Tsarism, 1914-1917* (London, 1977), p. 30.
13. While it is customary to stress the Tsar's unwillingness to cooperate with public institutions—including the Union of Zemstva and the Union of Towns, or the war-time creation, the War Industries Committees—one author has demonstrated that this was also the attitude of the Duma leadership in its relationship with these "public" organizations. See Pearson, *Russian Moderates*.
14. The latest, and among the most naive, of these works is by Alex de Jonge, *The Life and Times of Grigorii Rasputin* (New York, 1982), 368 pp. It was a History Book Club selection in 1982.
15. *The Letters of the Tsaritsa to the Tsar, 1914-1916* (London, 1923).
16. Liubosh, *Russkii fashist* (Leningrad, 1925). Additional information on Purishkevich's public and private activities can be found in: Hans Rogger, "Was There a Russian Fascism—The Union of Russian People," *Journal of Modern History*, XXXVI, 4 (1964), pp. 398-415; S. E. Kryzhanovskii, *Vospominaniia* (Berlin, 1938).
17. That this is indeed a diary was called into question at the time of its initial publication in 1924. See V. A. Malakov's letter to the editor below. The present edition of Purishkevich's diary is a translation of the 1924 edition published by Ya. Povolotsky in Paris.
18. The Liubosh study is the source of these claims; what makes them so suspect is that they seem to be consciously modeled on the career of Mussolini, down even to a physical description of Purishkevich which would have made him Il Duce's twin.
19. The two princely co-conspirators were Grand-Duke Dmitri Pavlovich (1891-1942), the Tsar's favorite cousin, and Prince Felix Yusupov (1887-1967), whose wife was the Tsar's niece.

# From the Diary of V. M. Purishkevich: The Murder of Rasputin

Translated from the Russian by Bella Costello

V. A. Maklakov
Paris

Dear Vasily Alexeyevich,

I am republishing the "Purishkevich Diary," which came out in 1918 in South Russia and which is devoted to the murder of Rasputin. The diary of a participant in the murder and, furthermore, one of such a character as was Purishkevich cannot fail to be of historical interest, particularly as it concerns one of the most fateful figures of the pre-revolutionary period—Rasputin, whose name was then on every Russian's lips. Judging from this diary, you, more than anyone else, may be in possession of certain details of this momentous affair. I am, therefore, addressing this request to you: Would you agree to *add* any facts to this present page of history which, for whatever reason, are not mentioned in the "Purishkevich Diary?" Or, at least, would you agree to give your opinion as to the degree to which Purishkevich's story corresponds to the truth?

I permit myself to hope that you will not refuse this request and thus will give to the future readers of the "Diary" and even to history the possibility of better understanding and more correctly evaluating the events of that time.

[signed] Ya. Povolotsky

Paris 1923

Ya. Povolotsky & Co.
Publishing House
Paris.

Dear Yakov Evgenievich,

Your letter poses various questions to which I could reply in various ways.

In the first place, you want me to *supplement* Purishkevich's diary. To this I cannot agree. The only facts I know are what others have told me. I never saw Rasputin and on the day of his murder I was in Moscow. All that I know about the murder, I know only from those who took part in it. These people are alive and if they wish can speak for themselves, as has Purishkevich. For me to speak *for them* would indeed be improper. As to "history," there my conscience is clear. Everything that I know has been put at the disposal of the investigator who conducted the inquiry into the murder of the Tsar,[1] and who broadened the field of his inquiry so far as to include the murder of Rasputin. This evidence of mine may also be of use to history in the future.

Of course this does not prevent me from answering your second question: Is Purishkevich's story true? However, it is not easy to answer this question *correctly*.

Of what truth are we speaking? If we are looking for *factual accuracy*, which would be so natural in a diary, then we would certainly fall into error. Purishkevich's diary is not a diary at all. It is merely the literary form he chose for his memoirs. That this is so hardly needs proving. It is obviously unlikely that amid the bustle of the period preceding the murder, Purishkevich could have found the leisure to write a diary—particularly one of such a form, i.e., not in the form of a simple recitation of the facts, but in the form of a tale with lyrical digressions, written in a bombastic and declamatory style. The very style shows us that what we have before us is not a diary, but "literature." I am further convinced that this is not a diary because I find in it such inaccuracies as are natural and unavoidable in memoirs, but which would be inexplicable in a diary. I can establish these in almost all cases

where I can check them personally, i.e., when they are
about me. Here are several examples:

Under 28 November, Purishkevich tells of how, with
Yusupov's agreement, he invited me to take part in the
murder; of how, on hearing his invitation, I "stared at
him," "was silent for a long time" and then refused; how
our talk ended with my asking him to send me a prearranged
telegram to Moscow with the news that the affair had been
successfully concluded, and even that I myself had fixed
the wording of the telegram. After this, according to
Purishkevich, he only sighed and "nothing remained for
him but to agree to my suggestion."

This story of Purishkevich's is a nonsensical mixture
of various conversations which took place at different
times and even with different people, about which Purishkevich could only have learned second hand. In trying to
remember what had happened, he obviously reconstructed
them from his memory and gave them the form of *one*
conversation between me and him. He failed to notice,
however, that such a transformation not only does not
correspond to reality, but even seems improbable. I
remember perfectly our first conversation and therefore
from this example I can see *how* Purishkevich wrote his
memoirs.

I remember his first approach to me and even my
surprise at it—a surprise related exclusively to the fact
that *Purishkevich* was in the plot. I had already heard about
the plot itself from *another* participant, whom I will not
name only because on principle I do not wish to name
anyone. In my conversation with that person my position
on the plot was not merely sceptical, it was unfavorable,
and our talk ended in a way that made it difficult to renew.
And so, on 28 November (I will accept Purishkevich's
date, though I do not remember myself) Purishkevich
informed me that he was also in the plot, and that only
highly principled people were involved in it. He added
that while he knew how opposed I had been to the original
plan, my objections had now been eliminated and that the

person who had spoken to me earlier had commissioned him, Purishkevich, to find out whether I would agree to reopening the conversation with him. There was no talk on that day of my *participation* in the murder, nor of my refusal to participate, nor, of course, of the sending of a telegram to Moscow (the idea of talking about this three weeks before the murder!). Purishkevich told me the names of the participants, the *day* of the murder and that was all. He did not even tell me *what* they wanted to discuss with me. But, in any case, I would never have talked to Purishkevich about it, since I did not consider him to be serious enough nor especially discreet enough for such an undertaking.

The conversation about a telegram took place much later in the following circumstances: On the day of the murder, as he indeed remembered, I had to be in Moscow where my public lecture on the peasant question had been arranged at the Law Society. The date had been fixed, notices had been sent out, and I had not the slightest reason to cancel the lecture. But, just before the murder, the participant, with whom I happened to talk, began to beg me urgently not to leave Petersburg on the day of the murder but to be there in case my advice might be needed. I will emphasize that, despite what Purishkevich said, I did not suggest at any time, to any of the participants, that I would be their *defender at a trial*. On the contrary, I argued definitively that a trial of Rasputin's murderers would be impossible in Russia—such a case would be too upsetting for Russia. But, on the other hand, to allow obvious murderers to go unpunished would also be impossible. Therefore, it was their duty to act in such a way that they would not be discovered. In essence, this would not be difficult, since the authorities, understanding the significance of the affair, would hardly try to find the murderers. They need only *make it possible* that they not be discovered. Therefore, the conspirators must refrain from any vainglorious urge to reveal themselves, must brag to no one, and on no account should they confess. From Purishkevich's diary, however, it is clear that he acted in just the opposite manner. A half-hour had not passed since the murder before he revealed himself to the police. This advice, not to give any clear evidence against themselves, was the reason why my presence as an adviser might have proved useful. Accordingly, I made an effort to put off my lecture in Moscow. I did wire my friend A. E. Vorms, who was then president of the Law Society. Since he did not know the cause of my request, he replied that it was absolutely impossible. I received his reply on the very day of my departure, i.e., on the eve of the murder.

I should have informed the conspirators of this reply, but on that day I could not get away from the Duma. I was to speak on behalf of the personnel committee on the question of the exclusion of deputy Lempitsky from the Duma. The debate on one of the previous reports had been unexpectedly prolonged and I could not leave or I would have risked losing my turn. I did not want to use the telephone either because the police were tapping all calls from the Duma. Late in the afternoon Purishkevich appeared at the Duma. I asked him to pass on to those concerned the message that I had not managed to postpone my meeting and that therefore I would be leaving. To this he replied with the unexpected information that the participants had decided that my presence in Petersburg at the time of the murder would be politically undesirable. The precise motive for this decision I have cited in my deposition at the inquiry and shall not state here. Then, as we were parting, I asked him to send me a telegram to Moscow if the affair ended successfully. He agreed to do this. We agreed on [the wording of] the text, and he carried out his promise: I received the telegram.

This is how things were and Purishkevich's account shows that his reminiscences are not a diary. If it were a diary, then the conversation about the telegram could only have been entered under 15 December and not under 28 November. There was no talk of this on the 28th. Likewise he could not have recorded my refusal to take part, even indirectly, in this affair on the 28th. I never discussed *this affair* at all with Purishkevich, unless you count my request to him to tell whoever it concerned that I *would be leaving*. But what Purishkevich wrote was not a diary, but memoirs. He remembered our conversations, which took place at various times, remembered as well what he had heard from others about my view of the affair, and out of all of this he concocted one conversation, arbitrarily placing it on 28 November, never realizing the resulting absurdity. I even think that when he was writing this, he was not free of the desire to put it in such a way as to justify his "sigh" and his conclusion: "typical kadet" [Constitutional Democrat]. At the time of writing his memoirs, Purishkevich was once again possessed by his old anti-kadetism.

The same inaccuracy and inconsistency is also found under 24 November. Purishkevich writes that on this day Yusupov showed him and the others the potassium cyanide (in both crystals and in solution) which he was supposed to have obtained from me. This is not true. It was not I who gave Yusupov potassium cyanide, or more precisely, what to Yusupov passed for potassium cyanide—had it been genuine no amount of hardiness on Rasputin's part would have saved him. But this assertion is absurd. How could I on the 28th of November have been invited for the first time to participate in the murder, as Purish-kevich says, if already on the 24th I had supplied them with potassium cyanide? This is, again, the result of "memoirs," natural forgetfulness, and careless exposition.

If such minor inaccuracies turn up in this very small number of cases where I am involved, it is difficult to suppose that he was any more accurate with the rest. It would therefore be a mistake to look for documentary truth in his diary. But this only applies to those details which might fade from memory. The main line of the narrative is nonetheless correct. So much rubbish, drawn from simple rumours and gossip, have been written about Rasputin's murder, that to hear the account of an eye-witness, even with those errors of detail inevitable in a memoir, is both interesting and useful.

However, accounts of contemporaries, and even more, those by participants, normally contain that relative truth which is usually called "historical." Such accounts are valuable not only for their truth, but also for their delusions. Even deliberate untruth can be characteristic and aid in an understanding of an era and its mood. From this viewpoint, Purishkevich's diary cannot but be interesting. There is only one reservation: He depicts boldly and vividly not so much the era as his own personality. For a judgment of the era and the people, one must not rely on his views and opinions—many of these are clearly nonsense. Purishkevich was a passionate and a biased man. He had no natural feeling for justice or tolerance. Moreover, his opinions, even the most basic ones, often changed. Nevertheless, Purishkevich himself played such an original and striking role in our social and political life that his personality merits interest if not study. However it is not so much his actual personality that is interesting as it is the *means* by which he achieved that resounding success he enjoyed in Russia. It would be difficult to deny that at a certain period he was nearly the most popular of people. True, this popularity was of a specific kind and would not have pleased everyone. But if Purishkevich were despised or even hated in certain intellectual and progressive circles, then the broad, apolitical masses, who only read the newspapers, and even for the most part those popular newspapers which mocked him in all kinds of ways, nevertheless had a friendly attitude towards him. If one takes into account *what* the Russian masses could have known about Purishkevich, *what sort of person* they could have imagined him to be, judging by the victories in the Duma for which he had become famous and from those political ideas which he supported in the Duma, then his success with the crowd presents an interesting psychological *riddle*. But his diary, with all its inaccuracies and declamations, even with its notorious share of posing, reveals in him certain qualities which were not at first obvious. They may even lead to some sort of explanation of the secret to his success. For now, when in the short interval since the revolution there have been so many idols who rose as quickly as they later fell, when in the very near future in Russia new leaders will be sought, the question of this secret is not void of interest.

I would hardly be mistaken in saying that public opinion of Purishkevich was not the same throughout those ten years in which he engaged public attention. Purishkevich before the war and Purishkevich during the war were two different people. Before the war his was a negative greatness. Some thought him irresponsible, while others considered that he was a conscious trouble-maker, but it is unlikely that anyone saw in him a serious and sincere statesman. Those very Duma scandals, on the basis of which he built himself a career, can only be explained by either a macchiavellian desire to discredit the Duma itself or by a morbid lack of equilibrium, linked to a vainglorious desire to get himself talked about. Had Purishkevich died before the war, the recollections preserved of him would have been of *such* a man, then his great popularity would have remained a simple illustration of our political backwardness, of the instinctive inclination of our people toward anarchy and disorder. But the war forced a change in the opinion of Purishkevich. It brought out traits in him hitherto unsuspected. It revealed, first of all, a passion which not only was stronger in him than all others, but perhaps even explained them, namely, patriotism. Purishkevich sacrificed to the war all the powers at his disposal—his political sympathies, personal biases, and even his own reputation. From the moment the war began he was transformed. He realized that everything which up to then had attracted public attention to himself and had aroused interest in him, i. e., his clamorous party activities, was bad for Russia. And, understanding this, he immediately stopped these activities. As he says in his diary, for the first three years of the war he was a political corpse. This is true. Previously his whole political life lay in the service of internal party dissensions. When he gave these up, his whole [political] life ended. With his whole being Purishkevich acknowledged the necessity of ending internal quarrels. Everyone called for this, but demanded it of *others*, not of *themselves*. Purishkevich made this demand in the first place of himself and fulfilled it honestly. Purishkevich's patriotism was also for him a genuine stimulus. The man who before the war had created nothing, but had only destroyed, criticized, and mocked, suddenly turned out to be an organizer. On his initiative a whole network of auxiliary aids for the army was established—supply centers, hospital trains, etc. Using his old contacts and his own fame, he obtained funds from sources inaccessible to others, found means for himself and his co-workers which would not have worked for others. In a word, he managed to press into service for the common cause all that capital he had acquired by *other*[2] means. This work engaged all of his attention and his interest and taught him the ways of social work. But the murder of Rasputin revealed in him yet another trait which had likewise been unknown. One can view this murder with any attitude one wishes, politically and morally. One may think it only did harm. One can be indignant about the fact or the form of the murder. But one thing cannot be denied: Purishkevich, in participating in the murder, gained nothing for himself. On the contrary, he risked everything. He even made this sacrifice for his country, not for himself. He could not have foreseen, of course, that this murder would be the first step towards revolution. For him personally, in any case, revolution would have meant ruin. It unleashed passions which for him with his political views would have been pitiless. But, one thing is clear: however one regards Purishkevich, even his worst enemies would not suppose that he could have gone into the service of the Bolsheviks, that he would have sold himself to them as did so many of those who had previously held the same views as he did. But Purishkevich would not have gained anything for himself even had he *secured* the goal which he had set himself—*the salvation of the monarchy by ridding it of Rasputin.* If he had, by means of this murder, succeeded in staving off the revolution and strengthening the shaky regime, then for such a service, the regime would have revenged itself on its deliverer. That personal position which Purishkevich had succeeded in reaching would in any case have been undermined by this. He would never have been *forgiven* for such a service. Therefore, by his participation in the murder Purishkevich proved his sincerity, his capability of sacrificing himself, his happiness, and his fate for the sake of Russia. Before the war this quality was not apparent in him, but perhaps herein lies the solution to the riddle of the special respect which Purishkevich was able to command among his political coterie. The mass of the people instinctively felt that he was moulded of a different clay from many of those defenders of the state and church who now, in Soviet Russia, are serving the new regime, not the people, who are reforming the church or the communists' police apparatus. And Purishkevich's diary, with its lyrical outpourings, its turbulent hatred of those he regards as Russia's enemies, its superficial and biased judgments of people, with its political naivete, verbose and disconnected, like his speeches in the Duma, provides us with not simply a basis on which we can learn *how* the murder was executed, but in addition, provides a key to an understanding of the disturbance in the hearts and minds of people then baffled by what was happening in Russia, and which explains this murder. His diary is a page of social pathology, and from this perspective is of historical interest.

However, to avoid falling into an error of perspective, one must also take into account the time when Purishkevich wrote his memoirs. If, as I suppose, he wrote his memoirs *much later than* the time of the murder, then his *later* moods were bound to be reflected in it. About these I can only conjecture. After the February Revolution, I saw little of Purishkevich, but from our meetings I got the impression that he was in much *the same frame of mind* as he had been in during the war. Of course, from his point of view he could only have a sharply negative attitude towards the Provisional Government, its policies, and its composition. But he did not fight it, nor did he rejoice in its failures, and did not say "the worse, the better." I met him once in Petersburg, when he had just returned from the station where he had witnessed scenes of anarchy, of which there were many at the railway stations: besieged trains, deserters from the front, disorder among soldiers over the new discipline. He did not gloat, he didn't even wash his hands of the whole business. "This is not the time to sort out who is responsible for what has happened," he said. "We must, come what may, support the Provisional Government as long as it does not lay down its arms to the enemy." I left Russia before the Bolshevik revolution and did not see Purishkevich again. I heard that he had been imprisoned in the Peter and Paul fortress, and that despite his odious name and the fact that he did not conceal his views, he received not only the respect but even the goodwill of the Red army soldiers. Then his case came up: in the court he was not cowardly, he did not repent and did not flatter the judges, as did many others. They gave him a comparatively light sentence and subsequently he escaped to the south. But when the Brest-Litovsk peace was signed and he realized that despite all the efforts and concessions Russia was beaten, that the revolution had *for the moment* completely failed, he became embittered, and returned to his old positions. He reproached the Whites for their half-measures, for not having unfurled their former banners, for not having spoken out to the very end. His death permitted him to miss seeing the collapse of the Whites, and he was not faced with the fatal question: *Which* is the right path, when *the path of the Whites too is closed?* But, at that time, when he was remembering the past, he judged it from his new position: in his diary no doubt he tried to see himself with that psychology which led him to take part in the murder of Rasputin. But, he was already seeing himself and others in the light of later events.

These then are the reservations which need to be borne in mind when assessing Purishkevich's version of what happened.

[signed]   V. Maklakov

Paris 1923

### Notes

1. Maklakov is referring to the Muraviev Commission report. See *Padenie tsarskogo rezhima*. 6 vol. Leningrad, 1924-1927. [Ed.]
2. An allusion to Purishkevich's supposed involvement with the Black Hundreds.

*19 November 1916*

I spent today in a state of great emotional excitement. For the first time in many years I experienced a feeling of moral satisfaction and the consciousness of a duty honestly and courageously fulfilled: I spoke in the Duma about the current conditions in Russia. I demanded that the Government tell the Tsar the truth about the state of things and, without any of the sly faces of the courtier, to warn the monarch of the danger with which Russia is being threatened by the dark forces which swarm throughout our home front—forces which are prepared to capitalize on the slightest mistake, failure, or blunder of his government in domestic matters, and to shoulder him with the responsibility for it—in these unendingly difficult war years of trial visited on Russia by the Almighty.

And what a lot of mistakes there are: *our government consists of one unrelieved kaleidoscope of mediocrity, egotism, and the pursuit of careers, of people who have forgotten their country and recall only their interests, living only for the present.*

How terribly sorry I am for the sovereign, who perpetually oscillates in his search for people capable of occupying a position at the helm of state, without ever finding any. And what a lot of wretches there are who, moved by ambition rather than any sense of responsibility for the posts they occupy, are willing in these crucial times to accept administrative positions for which they have neither experience nor talent.

During the two and a half years of war I have been a political corpse: I was silent. Even on the days of my chance visits to Petrograd to visit the Duma I sat at its meetings a simple spectator—someone without any political views. I thought then as I think now that all domestic quarrels should be forgotten in time of war, that all party differences should be set aside in the interests of that great common cause which, at the Tsar's call, long-suffering Russia demands of all her citizens. And only today, yes, only today did I permit myself to break my vow of silence. And, I broke it not for the sake of a political squabble, not to settle accounts with political opponents, but only in order to make it possible to reach the throne with those thoughts held by the broad Russian masses and with those bitter complaints heard throughout Russia—complaints which are accumulating and increasing every day over the whole expanse of Russia—[the people] can see no way out of the situation in which they have been put by the Tsar's ministers, those puppets whose strings are firmly held by Grigory Rasputin and the Empress Alexandra Fyodorovna, this evil genius of Russia and of the Tsar, the German woman who remains on the Russian throne, alien to the land and to the people whose example of solicitude and loving care she should have followed.[1]

It is hard to write these lines, but a diary brooks no lies. As a living witness of the mood of the Russian army from the first days of the Great War, I watched with feelings of the most profound bitterness as the authority and appeal of the Tsar's name grew daily weaker in the military units and, alas, not only among officers but also among the crowds of ordinary soldiers. There was but a single cause for this—Grigory Rasputin. His fatal influence on the Tsar through the Tsarina, and the Tsar's unwillingness to free himself and Russia from the participation of this dirty, depraved, and mercenary peasant in high state affairs, are pushing Russia into an abyss from which there is no return.

My God! What is obscuring the eyes of the Sovereign? What prevents him from seeing what is going on about him? His ministers, who hide the truth and, under the pressure of selfish interests, play with the fate of the dynasty are pathetic. When will there ever be an end to this?

What is it that makes Russian high officials and members of the Tsar's court remain silent? Cowardice. Yes, only gross cowardice and the fear of losing their positions. For this they sacrifice the interests of Russia. They are afraid to tell the Tsar the truth.

This was made clearer than ever to me on the 3rd of November when, returning with my train from the Rumanian front, I was invited by the Tsar to lunch at Mogilev[2] where I made a report to him about the mood of our armies at Rena, Brailov, and Galatz.

I remember clearly the brilliant and noisy crowd of Grand-dukes and generals who, before lunch, waiting with me for the Tsar to enter the dining room, exchanged their views on military events and on Russia's domestic scene. One after another, they came up and spoke to me: Will you tell the Tsar? Will you explain to him about the state of affairs? Tell him about Shturmer![3] Explain Rasputin's pernicious role! Draw his attention to the demoralizing influence of both of them on the country! Don't be afraid to lay it on thick. The Tsar will believe you, and your words will make the proper impression on him!

"Yes, your highness!" "Very well, General!", I replied to one after the other, to the right and to the left. But my heart grew heavier and sadder with each passing moment. How is this, I thought. Surely it is not my place, given that I have spent the entire war at the front, involved only in the military interests of our armies, to tell the Tsar about things which are *your* daily duty to tell him, you who are well acquainted with everything that Rasputin and his gang are up to and who know what they are doing to Russia, while hiding behind the name of the Tsar and destroying the love and respect for him in the eyes of the people.

Why do you remain silent? You, who see the Tsar daily, you who have access to him, who are close to him. Why do you push me on this path of revelation? I was invited by the Tsar for other purposes, and am so out of touch now with Russia's internal conditions, and with the policies pursued by these "caliphs for a day," those undistinguished ministers who make their appearance and then burst like soap bubbles.

Cowards! I thought then, and cowards I repeat with conviction now!

Miserable egoists who receive everything from the Tsar but who are incapable even of protecting him from the consequences of that fatal mist which obscures his mind's eye and prevents him, amid the intoxicating fumes of court flattery and governmental lying, from interpreting correctly the true feelings of his troubled people.

Thus I spoke the bitter truth to the Tsar then at Headquarters, and now to all of Russia in the Duma. As his true, incorruptible servant, sacrificing my own interests to the interests of the country, I illuminated that truth which had been concealed from him, but which has been and is seen by all of suffering Russia.

Yes, I expressed what undoubtedly is felt by the best Russian people, regardless of their party, tendency, or convictions. I understood this as I left the rostrum of the Duma after my two-hour speech. I understood it from the flood of greetings, handshakes, and the unfeigned delight that was apparent on all the faces of those who clustered around me after my speech—a crowd made up of representatives of all social classes, for the Taurida Palace on the 19th of November was filled to overflowing with what is called the flower of the nation, culturally, socially, and officially.

I know that I expressed what is felt by Russia, that Russia which, from the extreme right wing to those representatives of the left parties not bereft of a sense of the government's interests, equally evaluates the situation which has arisen, and equally regards that horror which is Rasputin, as an inextinguishable icon lamp in the Tsar's chambers.

Indeed, all those who were present today in the Taurida Palace—on the benches below and in the galleries—were in sympathy with me. And, in the whole Duma only three or four people, headed by Markov and Zamyslovsky,[4] remained aloof from the feeling which gripped us as we appealed to the Sovereign, begging him to rid himself and Russia of this new Egyptian plague which is Rasputin.

But what does it matter? Who, more than themselves do they harm—these patriots of the bureaucratic variety, who are ready to follow anyone in power and who lovingly cherish people such as Protopopov,[5] Shturmer, and Voyeikov[6] and company, knowing their worth, or rather, estimating their value in government according to the situation and the circumstances.

As I was leaving the Taurida Palace, tired and exhausted, and feeling weak after all the handshakes and the greetings, I was overtaken in the Catherine

Hall by Kaufmann-Turkestansky, the Chief Plenipotentiary of the Red Cross at the Tsar's Headquarters,
who was leaving for there the next day. Embracing
me, he said he would be sure to get a typed copy of
my speech and would hand it to the Tsar personally.

When I returned home my wife told me of
something curious that had happened:

After the conclusion of my speech, many ladies
from the highest Petrograd circles and from the
aristocracy came up to her, seated in the gallery, and
asked her to convey to me their sympathy with all
that I had said. Among these ladies was the Baroness
Ikskyul von Gildenbant, one of Rasputin's most
fervent admirers (he visited her salon often and was
much at home there). She asked my wife to give me
her warm greetings and to pass on to me her
"admiration" of my speech and urged that I accept
an invitation to dine with her and some of her friends
in the next few days.

We had a good laugh over this invitation, the aim
of which was immediately clear to me: the honorable
Baroness obviously wanted to bring me together
with Rasputin, being convinced that I, too, would
fall under his hypnotic spell and, after meeting him,
would become his fanatic admirer.

*20 November 1916*

All day today I had literally no peace as I sat at
home working at my desk. My telephone kept
ringing from morning to night. Both friends and
strangers called to express their sympathy with
everything I had said yesterday. I must admit that the
extent of this sympathy reached such a pitch that it

became unbearable to remain in my study. There is no situation more stupid than that of having to listen silently to a eulogy of oneself, not daring to interrupt the speaker as he sings one's praises. An endless stream of visitors left their visiting cards as a sign of sympathy. Among these was a mass from members of the State Council and, one that I greatly prized, from old Count S. D. Sheremetev,[7] a man I have always loved and respected as much as the late, lamented A. A. Naryshkin—both fearless warriors beyond reproach.

I was intrigued by one caller who announced himself as Prince Yusupov, Count Sumarokov-Elston. After the usual exchange of greetings, he (not content with this), asked if he could visit me as soon as possible in order to explain several points which were related, as he put it, to Rasputin's role at Court, and of which it was "awkward" to speak on the telephone.

I asked him to come tomorrow morning at nine o'clock. It will be interesting to find out what he wants to talk about and what he needs!

### 21 November 1916

Today at exactly nine o'clock in the morning Prince Yusupov arrived. He is a young man of about thirty, dressed in a page's uniform; evidently he is fulfilling his military obligation as an officer. I was very much taken with both his external appearance, which radiated inexpressible elegance and breeding, and particularly with his inner self-possession. This is obviously a man of great will and character—rare

qualities among Russians, especially those in aristo-
cratic circles.

He stayed for more than two hours.

"Your speech will not bring the results you
anticipate," he announced straight away. "The
Sovereign does not like having pressure brought to
bear on him, and Rasputin's importance, you must
realize, will not only not lessen but on the contrary,
will increase— thanks to his complete influence over
Alexandra Fyodorovna who, since the Sovereign is
at Headquarters engaged in military affairs, is really
governing the country."

"But what can be done?" I asked. He smiled
mysteriously, and looking at me with an unblinking
gaze, he muttered: "Get rid of Rasputin."

I laughed. "That's easy to say, but who will do
it?" I said. "There are no decisive people in Russia
now, only a government which, while it could do it,
and skillfully, only clings to Rasputin and guards him
as if he were the apple of its eye."

"Yes," Yusupov replied, "You can't depend on
the government, but all the same, people will be
found in Russia."

"You think so?"

"I am sure of it! And one of them stands before
you."

I jumped up and started to pace around the
room. "Listen, Your Excellency, this is no joking
matter. You have just told me what has been in my
mind for a long, long time. I understand, no less than
you do, that one Duma speech will not end this
sorrow, but a drowning man clutches at a straw, and I
clutched at it. The solution of which you speak is no
surprise to me, especially as a few years ago, when V.
A. Dedyulin was alive— he was, as you know, the

Palace Commandant—I went specifically to see him at Tsarskoe Selo (we were close friends), solely for the purpose of convincing him of the necessity of liquidating Rasputin immediately, for even then it was clear to me that Rasputin was a fatal individual for the dynasty and therefore for Russia."

"And, what came of that?" asked Yusupov.

"As you see, nothing. Rasputin is alive to this day. Dedyulin evidently didn't dare to try anything like this. The horror of it all is that many of our high officials, like Sabler,[8] Rayev,[9] Dobrovolsky,[10] Protopopov, Shturmer, and Voyeikov were building their careers on Rasputin, and the slightest blunder by anyone who wanted to rid Russia of this scum either would have cost him his head or would have greatly increased the reptile's importance at Court."

"You are right," Yusupov replied. "Do you know that Rasputin is being protected by detectives from three different agencies?"

"Really!"

"Yes. He is guarded by plainclothes detectives from the Ministry of the Imperial Palace—on the request of the Empress; by detectives from the Ministry of Internal Affairs; and by those from . . . you guess . . . ."

"I couldn't tell you."

"This will surprise you: Detectives supplied by the Banks."

. . . . . . . . .

I smiled. "Prince," I said, "I have stopped being surprised by anything that happens in Russia. For myself, I want nothing, I have no personal aim, and if you agree to take part in ridding Russia finally of

Rasputin, then here is my hand on it. Now, let's consider what we can do and then, if we can find a few more suitable people, we can carry out our plan. But, for the sake of secrecy, we should not use any of our servants."

"I can already introduce you to two other people," Yusupov responded animatedly, as he shook my hand.

"If you are free today, then come to my home. They will be there and you can meet them. We'll discuss the issue and if four of us is too few, then we can look for someone else from among our friends. At the same time, I will outline my plan, the feasibility of which depends entirely on Grigory Efimovich's [Rasputin's] state of mental composure, and on his willingness to come to my home some evening soon."

On this we parted.


*22 November 1916*

Yesterday evening I went to Yusupov's. When I arrived at eight o'clock he was still alone. Thirty minutes later, Lieutenant S. [Sukhotin], a young officer of the Preobrazhensky Regiment arrived. He appeared to be a slow-moving but forceful man. After another ten minutes a tall, stately, and handsome man flew into the room. I recognized immediately that he was the Grand-Duke Dmitri Pavlovich. We were introduced to each other, and without further ado, began to discuss how we could eliminate Rasputin.

"The Countess[11] is not in Petrograd now," our host, F. F. Yusupov told us. "She is in the Crimea, and hasn't the slightest intention of returning to

Petrograd. However, on my last visit with Rasputin I told him that she would be returning to the capital soon for a few days and that if he, Rasputin, wanted, I would arrange for him to meet her at my home one evening when she would be visiting my parents."

"Rasputin accepted this invitation with delight and asked only that he be notified in good time of the day on which the Countess would be here so that he, in his turn, could make sure that 'She,' that is, the Empress, wouldn't summon him to Tsarskoe Selo."

. . . . . . . . . . . . . . . . . . .

"As you can see, gentlemen," Yusupov added, "given these circumstances, finishing off Rasputin does not present any difficulties. The only questions that remain are: by what means do we get rid of him, how do we elude the detectives so that after Rasputin's death suspicion should not fall on us, and where will we dispose of his corpse?"

After a prolonged discussion of the questions put by Yusupov, we unanimously decided that poisoning was the only way to kill Rasputin. Yusupov's palace, which stands on the Moika canal, directly across from the Police Station, ruled out the use of a revolver. This was true even though Yusupov suggested that we deal with Rasputin in his private dining room—located in the cellar of the palace— to which he would bring him on the appointed evening.

At the same time, it became quite obvious that four people were not enough to successfully execute the agreed upon plan. Because of our unwillingness to involve any of the servants in the affair, and of the necessity for a reliable chauffeur (without which the whole plan would be impractical), I suggested that we should ask Dr. S. S. Lazovert, an old doctor who had served with me for two years in my military unit. My suggestion was accepted. After about a half an hour's talk of the political situation in Russia, we agreed to meet again on the 24th of November at ten o'clock in the evening on my train which was parked in the freight section of the Warsaw station. Then we parted. I intended to leave for Jassy on the Rumanian Front in the middle of December, once I had procured all the necessary supplies for my work in our army zone there.

*24 November 1916*

I spent all of today with Dr. Lazovert scouting around for all the supplies necessary for my train before the departure for the front. In addition I also spent some time at Red Cross Headquarters. The usual disorder reigns there. Everyone was involved in intrigues, the search for honors, and red tape—all to the detriment of the real work at hand.

At twelve o'clock I stopped by Prince Alexander Petrovich Oldenburgsky's place and, after the usual report, had lunch. From there I went on to the Duma. How profoundly I esteem this noble, pure, and honest old gentleman for the self-denial with which he serves the sacred cause of aiding the wounded. He reminds me of my father in character and in temperament, and I treat him with filial devotion and love. I know he loves me as well and trusts me completely. It is true that he has fits of anger. He is irascible, and is subject to bursts of momentary anger which sometimes lead him to foolish decisions of which he himself is later the first to repent and to apologize to anyone, no matter how insignificant, he has undeservedly offended or subjected to his sudden anger, for he is completely open-hearted and as pure as crystal. His noble heart seeks only the good. I don't know what would have become of medical affairs at the front if Prince Oldenburgsky did not occasionally act decisively to sharply chastise those who, from personal interest and the pursuit of rank and honors, take every possible measure to conceal deficits and scandals in the medical aid to our wounded and sick soldiers—deficits which would jump out and hit anyone who would look into our military medical affairs on the western and eastern fronts. Naturally, the Prince is surrounded by a whole horde of unscrupulous people: bribe-takers, rogues, and careerists, who find out his weak points and play on them. Much of what he does while costly is not worth a brass farthing because it is the result of bad advice. But all of that is a trifle compared with the benefits this venerable old man brings to the front. He overflows with youthful ardour and energy. His unbounded good-heartedness can be seen in the smile which appears on those rare occasions when he sees coming to fruition some plan he has entrusted to an honest man.

Today, while I was giving my report to the Prince, I had a very disagreeable encounter with one Dvukrayev, the chief inspector of the medical unit of the northern front. He is the right-hand man of Yevdokimov, who values this sort of young upstart.

Here, truly, was a trio that I would long since have hurled from the Tarpeian rock:[12] Yevdokimov, the chief medical inspector, and his two outrunners, Gyubenet of the western front and Dvukrayev of the northern. One simply cannot count all of the disasters they have caused our armies and the chief and most terrible of them is that they are always trying to disguise the truth and are forever putting a stick in the spokes of the Red Cross organizations at the front. They seem to regard any detachment outside their purview as a reproach, in that its work in evacuating and feeding the wounded does underscore their low productivity and the feeble organization of their work.

My clash with Dvukrayev concerned this, and it ended by my calling him a professional liar in front of the Prince. As a result, Dvukrayev challenged me to a duel, prudently adding the proviso that he would fight me once the war was over for now was not the time. For reply, I simply laughed in his face and said that I would not retract my words and advised him to spend more time thinking about the wounded than about the quickest way to get new decorations (these are already falling on him like raindrops because of his fictitious reports on the well-being of his medical unit on the northern front).

The Prince put an end to any further exchange of courtesies between us by coldly bidding Dvukrayev farewell and then he and I went to lunch.

What will happen next? I don't know, but in all probability Dvukrayev will attempt to prevent me from visiting the northern front. In his opinion, I see things I ought not to see and cannot reconcile myself to his system of covering up scandals and proceeding under the slogan: "All is well."

I did not return to my train at the Warsaw Station until eight o'clock in the evening, whereupon I went to the library coach to make certain that everything was ready for our meeting set for ten o'clock.

. . . . . . . . . .

*24 November 1916*

Having permitted the orderlies and the drivers to leave the train, I drew the curtains in the library coach and waited. At exactly ten o'clock Dmitri Pavlovich arrived with Yusupov and Lieutenant S. in his private car.

I introduced them to Dr. Lazovert and we settled down to a further discussion of our plan. At this point Prince Yusupov showed us some potassium cyanide which he had obtained from V. Maklakov.[13] Some of this was in the form of crystals and some in a solution contained in a small phial which he continued to shake during the whole time he was in the coach.

Our conversation lasted almost two hours and together we worked out the following plan: On the appointed day, or rather night, we would all meet at Yusupov's at precisely midnight. At 12:30, having completed all the necessary preparations in Yusupov's dining room in the lower storey of the palace, we would go up to his study. At approximately one o'clock Yusupov would leave in my car to pick up Rasputin at Gorokhovaya.[14] Dr. Lazovert would be his chauffeur.

. . . . . . . . . . . . . . . . . .

Having brought Rasputin to his house, Yusupov would lead him directly into the dining room from the courtyard. To allow for this, the chauffeur was to park the car close to the entrance in such a way that when the car door was opened no silhouettes would be visible through the fence railings to any passerby, either on this side of the Moika or on the other, where, at No. 61, the police station was located. It was also possible that there might be spies wandering about, for we did not know how closely Rasputin was watched or even if they might not be posted around the place where he planned to spend a good half the night.

Once Dr. Lazovert had delivered Rasputin, he was to remove his chauffeur's uniform and climb the spiral staircase, which led from the entrance, past the dining room, and go to the Prince's drawing room where he would join us, that is, Dmitri Pavlovich, me and [Lieutenant] S. Together, we would take up our position at the top of the staircase, ready to go to Yusupov's aid down below in the event that things did not go according to our plan.

After Rasputin was dead, which in our opinion would be in ten or fifteen minutes after his arrival (depending on how much of the poisoned Madeira he drank), Prince Yusupov would come up to join us. We would then all go back down to the dining room where we would make a bundle of as many of Rasputin's clothes as we could. These we would give to Lieutenant S. who would put on Rasputin's overcoat (given his build and height, S. could be mistaken for Rasputin by the spies we still worried about, especially if he kept his face covered with the upturned collar) and go out into the courtyard to the car with the Grand-Duke and Lazovert who would again act as the chauffeur. They would then drive to my train at the Warsaw Station where, by that time, a hot fire should be burning in the stove in my passenger car. My wife and Dr. Lazovert's wife would burn all of Rasputin's clothes that the Grand-Duke and [Lieutenant] S. had brought in this. Then Dr. Lazovert and his passengers would load my car onto the supply wagon connected to my train and they would all then go by taxi or by foot to the Grand-Duke Sergei Alexandrovich's palace on the Nevsky. From there they would drive to Yusupov's palace on the Moika, and entering into the courtyard, would again park the car flat against the house, and come up to the drawing room where Yusupov and I would be waiting for them.

All of us would immediately go down to the dining room where we would wrap the corpse in some suitable material and, taking the "mummy" in the Grand-Duke's car, we would drive to some prearranged spot and drop it into the water, bound in chains and two-pood weights to prevent it from resurfacing through a hole in the ice. This seemed hardly possible because after the heavy frost everything in Petrograd—rivers, streams, and canals—was covered in thick layers of ice, and we would have to search for some place that was free of an icy crust into which we could drop Rasputin's body. Having decided on this, our meeting ended.

We decided to meet at my train again at ten in the evening on the first of December to work out any additional details. Before this we were to reconnoitre Petrograd for places which might be suitable for Rasputin's watery burial. To avoid involving our soldier drivers we decided that Dr. Lazovert would drive me in my car and that Yusupov would go in the Grand-Duke's car with Dmitri Pavlovich driving.

At twelve midnight we took a final leave of each other and left for our separate dwellings. I had taken on myself the task of buying the chains and weights at the Alexandrov Market for the plan we had concocted.

## 26 November 1916

Today was another day of kaleidoscopic impressions beginning in the very morning. I was sitting, sorting my mail, when a ring at the door brought me a packet from Professor Levashov, the chairman of the Council of the Pravye faction.[15] I opened it to discover that it was a request that I return to the lap of the Pravye, in which I had served as a member of the Council up to the 18th of November (the eve of my Duma speech) when I had severed all connections with it. The motive [of the request]: In such difficult times as these, people like me are especially valuable to the faction. I read the note, folded it, and put it away. I felt terribly hurt, bitter, and offended.

Reading between the lines I was able to understand what had led Levashov, Markov, and company to call on me to return. It was quite simple. These gentlemen had seen that my speech to the Duma on the 19th of November reflected the thoughts and feelings of all the honest people of Russia, of all patriotic-minded Russians, regardless of party or tendency. The Markovs, Zamyslovskys and Levashovs realized that their troika, which cringes before whoever happens to be in power, was isolated in Russia, that Russian rightists followed me, not them, and that it was I, not they, who appeared to express the desires and aspirations of the Russian people. They had licked the boots of Protopopov and had become his ardent admirers as soon as this rogue had become, to the sorrow of the Tsar and Russia, the Minister of Internal Affairs, and had supported their mediocre journal *Zemshchina* which was incapable of undertaking a critique of the government, but instead gazed ingratiatingly at the hands of the Minister of Internal Affairs as he fed them from the state coffers —their payments determined by the degree of devotion and the servility of their scribblers to the Minister of Internal Affairs.

How well I remember the last meeting of the faction before my speech. The meeting took place on the 18th of November in our faction's committee room, No. 36 in the Duma. I concisely outlined my entire speech to the faction and asked them to allow me to speak in their name in the Duma. This honor was denied to me.

I saw by their expressions that three-quarters of those present were my ardent supporters. But, is our faction really free to express its opinions? For the most part it is terrorized by Markov who, together with Zamyslovsky, prevent it from thinking independently and honestly, but turns it, especially the peasant delegates, into a type of Duma sheep. On those rare occasions when even this flock gets indignant and wants to think for itself, they threaten its members by saying that if there is an anti-government vote, the Duma will be dismissed and the responsibility for its prorogation will fall on the faction's members who, with their vote, gave a majority to those who oppose the views of the government. At this point, the peasant delegates, to avoid making a false step or to prevent the loss of the title of Duma delegate, yield to the Markovian arguments and become the pawns in his [Markov's] game of serving the government.

No! For me, such a policy, the policy of the so-called right, is an orientation, as they say, for the pocket book. It is thoroughly repugnant to me, and I certainly cannot reconcile with them or agree to have my ideals of government sullied by people whose conception of Russia is personified by decorated, uniformed rascals who speak in Russia's name from any responsible ministerial post they have managed to reach, who swindle the Sovereign and squander governmental funds. As a man of the right, I feel compelled to expose such men mercilessly, and their exposure will be understandable to all honest Russians, not as an attempt to discredit the Government, but as an effort to render it fundamentally healthy and to prevent others from clinging to the helm of the ship of state.

Such were the thoughts which spun like a whirlwind around my head today after I had read the invitation from the faction to return to its womb. It goes without saying that I will leave this appeal unanswered. The path of Markov, Zamyslovsky, and Levashov is not mine.

In any event, it is unlikely that we will get together again, either in the future or especially now, in these difficult wars years, when all energies should be applied to the spiritual unification of all Russian citizens regardless of their nationality or religious beliefs. There is only one question for each: "Do you love Russia and the Sovereign, and do you sincerely want to see the victory of our arms over the determined and powerful enemy?"

At a time when Russia should be seen with the vision of Ivan the Great,[16] Markov and Zamyslovsky, with their fractional blinders, cannot see beyond their own parochial interests. Much has to be forgotten and forgiven, and many sincere reconciliations must be made in the cause of a common love for our homeland . . . .

About twelve noon I received a telephone call from the palace of the Grand-Duke Kirill Vladimirovich informing me that His Highness had asked that I visit him on important business at about two o'clock today.

I replied that I would and decided that I would go, even though the Grand-Duke Kirill, like both his dear brothers, has always provoked in me a feeling of profound disgust. As for their mother, the Grand-Duchess Marya Pavlovna, from the very first days of the war, I could not bear to hear her name mentioned at the front.

I feel that the Vladimiroviches, and their mother, while remaining inherently foreign and germanophilic, do not only harm to our army at the front, but constantly intrigue against the Sovereign (which they try to disguise with high-flown talk about the good of Russia).

They have never given up their hope that the throne of Russia would one day revert to their line. I can't help but remember the story told by Ivan Grigorievich Shcheglovitov, of how, when he was Minister of Justice, Grand-Duke Boris Vladimirovich came up to him one day to have him elucidate the question: did they, the Vladimiroviches, have the right, according to the laws of the Russian Empire, to succeed to the throne, and if not, why not?

Shcheglovitov, who after this talk with the Grand-Duke Boris, became the subject of their cruel hatred, received from them the nickname of Vanka Cain,[17] explained to the Grand-Duke that they had no right to the succession because the Grand-Duchess Marya Pavlovna, their mother, had remained a Lutheran after her marriage.

Boris went off disappointed, but some time later he put at Shcheglovitov's disposal a document which made it clear that Marya Pavlovna had ceased being a Lutheran and had become a member of the Orthodox Church . . .

At two o'clock I arrived at the entrance of Grand-Duke Kirill's palace on Glinka Street and after several minutes was received by him. The official reason for inviting me, as I gathered from his first words, was that his wife Victoria Fyodorovna, a very pleasant and clever woman and the sister of the Rumanian Queen Marya, wished to give me some commissions for the Rumanian Queen since I was going with my hospital train to the Rumanian front through Jassy. But this was really only the Grand-Duke's pretext for our meeting and he was obviously after something else. He apparently wanted me to enlighten him about the mood of the social circles in which I moved and, along the way, he wanted to find out whether I was opposed only to the government of the Emperor or whether my opposition went deeper.

Apparently my drift did not satisfy him. He realized that it would not do to discuss or to condemn the Sovereign to me and he very quickly cut short the conversation which he himself had begun on this subject.

I then went with him to Victoria Fyodorovna and, after spending a quarter of an hour with her, I promised to send my wife to her, as the Grand-Duchess wanted her to buy a few things for the Rumanian Queen.

As I was leaving the Grand-Duke's palace, I became firmly convinced (in reviewing our conversation) that he, along with Guchkov[18] and Rodzianko[19] were plotting something which from my point of view was impermissible with regard to the Sovereign. But exactly what, I could not make out.[20]

## 28 November 1916

After having spoken with Yusupov on the telephone, I drove to his place today at one o'clock so that he and I could examine the basement of his palace which was to be the arena of our activities on the day of Rasputin's liquidation.

I drove in by the main entrance and went to the Prince's study through a veritable formation of his servants who were milling around his hallway.

"Listen, Prince," I said, "Surely this whole gang sitting in your hallway, headed by that liveried blackamoor, won't be around on the night of our reception for Rasputin?"

He began to laugh. "No," he said, "Don't worry, there will only be two men on duty at the main entrance, and all the rest will be given leave, including the blackamoor."

Yusupov and I went to the dining room which, as I said, is located in the lower level of his palace. Some workmen were there installing electricity. The dining room was still a mess. It was being completely remodeled, but it appeared to be a very suitable and remote setting for receiving our dear guest. Judging from the thickness of the walls, it seemed to me that even if shots had to be fired from there, the sound of their report would not be heard in the street. Even the windows, of which there are only two, are very small and barely reach the level of the pavement.

After examining the room, we went upstairs again to the Prince's sitting room and a quarter of an hour later I went to the Duma with the aim of meeting V. A. Maklakov. It seemed to Yusupov and me that his closer participation would be useful to our undertaking, even if Yusupov did not think that Maklakov would agree to an active role.

---

I found Maklakov in the Duma and, as the saying goes, immediately took the bull by the horns and, sitting down with him by the bust of Emperor Alexander II, told him that our numbers were insufficient for the success of our undertaking and that we really wanted him to participate in our final meeting and in the execution of the projected plan.

Maklakov stared at me fixedly and, after a long silence, he declared that he could hardly be of use as an active participant in Rasputin's actual liquidation, but that after it, if anything went wrong and we got caught, he would not only be prepared to help us with legal advice, but would willingly defend us in court, if it came to that.

At the same time, having sounded me out on the approximate date on which we were to accomplish our goal, he announced, joyfully it seemed, that quite independently of his wishes, he absolutely could not be our closer collaborator because he would have to be in Moscow for about a week at that time.

Then he added animatedly, "But I urge you, if the affair is successful, then please send me an express telegram, even if it only says: 'When are you arriving?' I shall understand that Rasputin is no more and that Russia can breathe freely."

I sighed. A typical "Kadet," I thought, but there was nothing to do but to agree to his request, and with that we parted.

## 29 November 1916

This morning was a busy one. First, I went with my wife by cab to the Alexandrov Market to buy weights and chains. We then brought them onto the train very cautiously to avoid arousing the curiosity of our train's crew, and hid them, partly in the pharmacy and partly behind the books in the library coach. Then at one o'clock, after having had lunch, Lazovert and I went off in my car to scout the outskirts of Petrograd, in accordance with the decisions of our last meeting.

Lazovert drove and we rode around for almost four hours in the bitter cold, examining every ice-hole in the Neva and in the little streams and bogs around Petrograd, evaluating their usefulness to our purpose. We returned home around five o'clock, shivering and numb with the cold, and were barely able to warm ourselves with the help of large doses of *tincturae coniaci*.[21] In the end, only two of the places we had examined seemed really suitable. One was a small ice-hole in a canal running from the Fontanka to the Tsarskoe-Selo Station which was badly lit at night. The other was outside the city limits on the old Nevka by the bridge leading to the islands.

I wonder what Yusupov and the Grand-Duke had found, and whether their attention had been drawn to these same ice-holes?

. . . . . . . . .

*30 November 1916*

I saw the costume Dr. Lazovert acquired today
on my orders for 600 rubles: a chauffeur's fur coat, a
sort of Astrakhan cap with ear flaps, and chauffeur's
gloves.

Lazovert modeled all of these for me, looking
like a typical chauffeur—foppish and impudent. For
the time being he took all these purchases to the
Astoria Hotel, where he stays during our visits to
Petrograd.

. . . . . . . . . . . . . .

*1 December 1916*

It is now one o'clock in the morning. The
Grand-Duke, Yusupov, and Lieutenant S. have just
left my train.

We have been working out the last details of our
plan. Yusupov and I would have liked to advance the
date of its execution and finish everything not later
than 12 December, but it turns out that the Grand-
Duke Dmitri Pavlovich has all his evenings engaged
right up to 16 December and on the evening which,
according to Yusupov, would have been the most
suitable for carrying out our plan, Dmitri Pavlovich
has some sort of feast with the officers of his
regiment and could neither cancel nor postpone it
since he himself had fixed the day of this gathering
and any change in schedule might raise speculation.

From what Yusupov said I understood that Rasputin had shown considerable impatience about being introduced to the lady in whom he was interested, and had reminded him [of his promise] and pressed him not to put it off.

Yusupov had recently been at Rasputin's and had told him that he would tell him in advance of the day of the meeting, but that he could not set the exact day yet, because the Countess, who interested Grigory Yefimovich, had yet to arrive and would travel to Tsarskoe Selo via Petrograd not before the middle of December.

"I stopped by Rasputin's," Yusupov informed us, "mainly to find out whether Rasputin, in leaving for one of his nocturnal escapades, generally tells his police spies where he intends to spend the night and in particular whether he intends to tell them that he will be visiting me."

"Unfortunately," the Prince added, "this question remains open, for neither Rasputin nor his loving secretary, fraulein Golovina,[22] who is at Rasputin's apartment practically twenty-four hours a day, gave me a definite reply."

"What is his attitude toward you, Felix?" the Grand-Duke asked. "Does he trust you?"

Yusupov burst out laughing. "Oh, completely! I am above suspicion. He likes me very much. He even regrets that I don't hold an administrative post and promises to make me into a great statesman."

"And what did you say to that? . . ." The Grand-Duke asked, throwing him a meaningful look while taking a drag on his cigarette.

"I?" replied Yusupov, who lowered his gaze and, fluttering his eyelashes, assumed an ironically languid look, "I modestly informed him that I consider myself too young, inexperienced, and un-prepared for service in the administrative field, but that I was gratified beyond belief that one so well known for his perspicacity as Grigory Yefimovich should have such a flattering opinion of me."

We all burst out laughing.

"C'est ravissant, mais c'est vraiment ravissant!" the Grand-Duke exclaimed several times.

. . . . . . . . . .

Just before the conclusion of our meeting we decided that, in the event that Rasputin should inform his police spies of his planned whereabouts on the evening of his visit to Yusupov's palace, we would deflect their suspicions by doing the following: Rasputin, as is well known, spends most of his nights in drinking bouts with women of easy virtue at the Villa Rodé. He is regarded as a regular there, and all the waiters know him well. Therefore, we decided that after Rasputin was dead and the Grand-Duke and Lieutenant S. had gone to my train to burn the dead man's clothes, the Lieutenant would call the Villa Rodé from a telephone booth in the Warsaw Station and asking for the manager would inquire: "Has Grigory Yefimovich arrived yet? Is he there? In which room?"

Having waited for the reply, which would naturally be negative, [Lieutenant] S., just before putting down the receiver, would say as if to himself, but making certain that the manager of the Villa Rodé heard him: "Aha! So he's not there yet. Well, that means he'll be arriving any minute!"

. . . . . . . . . . . . . . . .

We thought this necessary in the event that clues to Rasputin's disappearance should lead to an investigation at Yusupov's palace. We had a ready answer: "Yes, Rasputin was here, he spent part of the evening with us and then said he was going to the Villa Rodé." Naturally the authorities would then turn to the management of the Villa Rodé with the question: Had Rasputin been there? And, it would immediately become clear that inquiries had been made about him; that someone had asked when he was to arrive. If Rasputin had not arrived but instead had disappeared, then that was not our fault but Grigory Yefimovich's. Obviously he had chosen other companions for his revelries—companions unknown either to us or to the police.

As we were leaving we decided to fix the night of 16-17 December for carrying out our plan and, in order to avoid arousing any possible suspicion, to meet only one more time at Yusupov's on the 13th or 14th of December. Also we would greet each other by telephone with the words "Vanya has arrived."

### 4 December 1916

This morning I received a note from the very charming B. B. Glinsky, the editor of *The Historical Herald*,[23] asking me to be sure to attend the meeting of the Society of the Russian State Map, of which I am president and he is co-president.

The meeting is tomorrow at 8:30 at the Economics Club on Samsonyevsky Street. I sent a reply to Glinsky to assure him that I would certainly be there.

As I read Glinsky's note, I was involuntarily reminded of the history of the origins of this society, which I had founded in the most difficult of circumstances.

My God! What tribulations have to be endured in Russia to give birth to pure, good, national, and patriotic institutions. Any Kadet can try to start an organization, and the authorities, out of a fear of being considered reactionary, will approve it—no matter that it is the most absurd or anti-governmental institution or organization imaginable. But, if the right should apply to the authorities—and it is much harder to stir the right into action than the left—then the right can expect nothing from the government but obstacles, impediments, and sticks in the wheel. It is worth pondering on what is being done to our people who are being preeducated by the "Educational League" and its teachers and textbooks, by Kadets, the most pernicious party in Russia; an ever-smoldering hotbed of Russian revolution. And, does the government combat this? Not at all! And if it does attempt to, it only does so by issuing lifeless circulars from the Ministry of Education. Do not expect anything fresh or lively from that source. Incidentally, the character of our state education carries within itself the seeds of its blossoming as well as of its destruction. Thus, the authorities furiously slashed and mutilated the regulations which I had drawn up for the Filaretov Society of Public Education, the aim of which was to have been an active struggle in deeds, not words, against the corruption of the Educational League—for whom the education of the people is not a goal but simply a means for attaining their criminal end: revolutionizing the masses. Thus it is for everything. What it cost me to gain approval of The Russian State Map Society's charter!

One might have thought that this was a more patriotic, a more responsible time! But, no! Months passed in official red-tape and the governmental *veto* hung like the sword of Damocles over my project. Meanwhile, the whole of Germany is covered with a network of societies like the one I planned, even though they are infinitely less necessary there than here in Russia. The German Government, and to some extent the Ministry of Foreign Affairs in Germany, are possessed of a nationality, whereas our rulers and Zeuses, who have been sitting in state by the Moika since the time of Nesselrode,[24] have with rare exceptions long since forgotten their nationality and the interests they represent. They are concerned only with the beauty of the style, à la Gorchakov,[25] of the letters and diplomatic notes which they produce artistically in French, not without a sprinkling of Bilibinish wit.[26] Russia and her interests are their least concern, and any Englishman, or German, and now even Japanese, having thoroughly befogged a Russian diplomat, can twist him around his little finger and make him give up Russia's vital interests and needs at any time.

How well I remember my visit to Shturmer on the islands (as Prime Minister he was living in the Elagin Palace) during one of my trips to Petrograd from the front. Shturmer received me cordially, but he made an incredibly wry face when I explained to him (with due caution so as not to offend our Minister of Foreign Affairs), the task and goals of the projected society.

"Germany," I told Shturmer, "is covered by a network of similar organizations whose task is to

97

provide the population with the outlines of Germany's future boundaries, on the north, south, east, and west, once a victorious war has been concluded."

"The society which I am founding will include writers, scientists, publicists, and professors from all parties and groups, and will have the similar aim of outlining to the Russian people Russia's future boundaries and of providing a good grounding in the historical, geographical, and ethnographical bases of her future borders. That way, once peace has been concluded, the Russian people will know what they have the right to demand and Russian diplomacy, in its claims to this or that territory, will be able to rely on the support of the Russian people who have made such sacrifices to the homeland in the years of war, by virtue of their sacrifices, they have the moral right to be the conscious inspirers of Russian diplomacy— a diplomacy which, supported by the will of the people, will be able to speak more firmly at the peace conference, secure in that authority which should be characteristic of Russia's representatives.

Shturmer listened to me and when I had finished, he declared: "Of course, V. M., this Society can't do any harm, although at the time of the peace talks, it might be a sort of controlling body over the Diplomatic Department of which I am the head. But, I really do not see the essential usefulness of such a society. The fact is," he added significantly, "that I, as Minister of Foreign Affairs, have already called on Professor Dmitri Ivanovich Ilovaisky to outline a plan of our territorial claims in the West for me, so that I can appear at the peace talks fully armed."

Despite the seriousness of the subject of our conversation, I could not help smiling at the mention of D. I. Ilovaisky, to whom Shturmer had assigned the part of the nymph Egeria[27] to his own role in foreign affairs. Could one really imagine a more pitiful role for the Russian plenipotentiary at the forthcoming peace congress than to have to rely on eighty-year-old D. I. Ilovaisky, almost in his second childhood and clearly incapable of orienting himself in modern European affairs or understanding the part that Russia, as a Slavic power, will have to play among the peoples of Europe at the end of the world war.

Shturmer and I parted more coolly than we had met, and only a few months later, thanks to the good offices of my assistant in the Duma and of my friend, A. N. Khvostov, [28] did I succeed in establishing the statutes of my "Society of the State Map." It has become an extremely vital body and has attracted the most distinguished representatives of all trends of our social and political thought.

These were the memories which my reading Glinsky's invitation to tomorrow's meeting of the society evoked . . . .

I spent the entire day travelling around on business connected with the provisioning of my train. It must arrive in Rumania impeccably equipped for they say that our army there is in need of absolutely everything.

I obtained: boots for the soldiers, thanks to the good offices of Prince Oldenburgsky; invaluable medicines given to me by the Americans; piles of linens which I obtained from Countess Musin-Pushkin; and finally, for the library coach, a whole series of Russian and foreign classics and other books for the soldiers which I will distribute to the regiments in the field.

I got home late, incredibly tired, but infinitely happy with my success in this assignment.

As usual in the evening, I read Horace's *Odes* in the original, in which I find ever newer beauties each time. I do not think that I could ever get bored with them. How delightful, for example is the ode:

*Odi profanum vulgus et arceo*[29] or: *O navis referent in mare te novi fluctus*!

What a pity that Latin, that language of the gods, is so neglected in our secondary schools!

## 5 December 1916

This morning as usual I went to the Duma to get my mail, for if you get behind two or three days, so many letters from all over Russia pile up that you cannot make sense of them and sometimes miss the important things through a careless reading.

I got into a conversation with the Duma member Count Kapnist who was on his way to a meeting of some Duma committee. As usual, the subject that is now horrifying Russia came up—the policies of Protopopov.

"No, Count," I said, "I am not at all surprised that Protopopov was offered the post of Minister of the Interior, but only that he accepted it. Whatever you may think of him, he seems to be a bright fellow and must realize that with his administrative experience he should not be guiding the ship of the Russian state at a time like this."

"You don't know him very well," Kapnist replied hotly. "In the first place, he is extremely self-confident and second, he is ambitious. Just listen to what he said to me recently when I reproached him for being out of place":

'Yes, talk, it's easy for you to talk. You're a Count, you are Kapnist. You are rich, you're rolling in it. You want for nothing. When I was young, I used to give lessons for fifty kopecks an hour, and as far as I am concerned the post of Minister of the Interior is one that you don't need.'

"So!" Kapnist added, "How do you like that for an ideology?"

I shrugged my shoulders. "Vulgar fellow! He obviously thinks that ministerial posts should fall to those who have made their way in the world, regardless of their talents, and that these should be compensation for fate's earlier neglect."

In the afternoon I drove to the Moika to the Empress's Linen Storehouse, which is operated by the War Minister's wife, Sukhomlinova. The fact is that baths for the soldiers are being organized in my main detachments at the front and therefore, however much linen is brought from Petrograd, it never seems to be enough.

I cannot stand Sukhomlinova. She seems to me to be an international adventuress like Maria Tarnovskaya. But, business first and, as they say, even a mangy sheep provides some wool.

Six months ago my sister, who had been working in the Empress's Storehouse at the Winter Palace and who had only given up the work when the common tongue had become almost exclusively German, advised me to contact the directress of the Storehouse, Princess Obolenskaya, and ask her to give me a certain quantity of linen. I followed her advice and, at the direction of Princess Obolenskaya, sent a telegram to the Empress Alexandra Fyodorovna in which I set forth my request. But, as I should have expected (I was hoping that the affair would be arranged without the Empress but be limited to a simple order from Obolenskaya) Alexandra Fyodorovna, who detests me, refused my request. I was informed of this by Count Rostovtsev.

The reply was very offensive for it said that the Empress sends linen regularly to the army through her own couriers.

What a fool I was, I thought, to send a request to Alexandra Fyodorovna, even if it was not for myself. Her couriers really do bring linen to the army, but they distribute it to the rear units which are up to their ears in all sorts of supplies— to the detriment of the barefooted and hungry front supplied exclusively by me. I alone am responsible for supplying medicines, linens, boots, tobacco, and books to the trenches.

Working under Sukhomlinova on the Moika is a whole hive of ladies, young and old. The work is evidently going well, but what is distasteful is the infinite number of rear ensigns, hastily promoted from rich families of various ranks, who have found a perch here as adjutants, goodness knows on whose instructions. They all march around in service tunics although they have never smelled gunpowder and never will.

Occasionally War Minister Sukhomlinov comes into the Storehouse, ceremoniously wearing a short, tight, double-breasted jacket. Judging by the way his wife treats him, he is clearly extremely subordinate to her and certainly sees everything through her eyes.

Having managed to obtain some linen from Sukhomlinova, I drove off to see Prince Oldenburgsky on very important business. The Russian army had recently suffered heavy losses on all fronts from German poison gases. At the front I had discovered one of the reasons for this horrible phenomenon: it is because our worthy commissariat periodically sends the regiments only just enough "Zelinsky" gas masks, i.e., exactly the same number as there are soldiers in the regiment, not even allowing the regiments a minimal reserve of masks.

As a result, this is what happens: one day a regiment of 4,000 men receives, let us say, 4,000 gas masks which are distributed to all ranks as part of their equipment. The next day there is a battle and the regiment loses a third or a quarter of its number on the battlefield. A week later reinforcements arrive, but they cannot be issued gas masks and when the regimental commander asks for supplies on the basis of his register they reply, taking no notice of the military action of the regiment during this time, "Your regiment was fully supplied with gas masks on such and such a date and we cannot give you any more now unless we withhold them from other units." Today this letter arrives and the next day the Germans exterminate the newly arrived reinforcements, who have no gas masks, with their poison gas.

Prince Oldenburgsky showed deep concern over this and promised to obtain for me, by dint of application in the proper quarter, 25,000 Zelinsky gas masks for distribution where necessary at the front. Apart from this, he would also give orders to the commissariat that in the future, masks should be sent to regiments along with reinforcements.

I did not get home until seven o'clock. I dined, and at half past eight arrived at the meeting of the Russian State Map Society.

Glinsky wanted me, the President of the Society, to preside at the meeting, but I declined. As a man of too definite political views, known to be of the extreme right, I do not like to frighten away from the organization that I founded intelligent and useful people, even if they lack political courage. Therefore, I am prepared to do any hard work in connection with this business that I am getting underway, but I will always leave the front pew and conspicuous roles to those who are willing and able to perform them, but whose political views are not as definite or as glaring as mine. Being free of petty ambition, I see how the work that I began is advancing, not by frightening people away, but by attracting other useful and necessary people to the Society.

Because today's meeting was a joint meeting of the sections of the Society dealing with the Persian, Turkish, Austrian, and German frontiers, there were many people present. I saw A. A. Bashmakov, D. I. Vergun, Professor F. I. Uspensky, Professor Zhilin, A. F. Vasilyev, and many others unknown to me, civilians and soldiers with Generals' braids whose names I did not learn. The fact is, that many useful people are co-opted as representatives of the sections who are active workers and experts in their fields, but it is too hard for me to remember them all.

The meeting began to drag. It was extremely interesting, but what I dislike is the habit of some of our experts of delivering long speeches, on questions which are clear to everyone present, which have the single aim of showing off their knowledge.

The Russian, the average Russian who makes Russia's history, is a curious creature. He can never completely achieve realistic results in his undertakings, for nothing is ever enough for him and he always goes to extremes. In Russia there is no better way of ruining some project which has been well and soundly planned and firmly based, than to propose something beyond what is aimed at. A crowd, and not even a simple crowd but an intelligent one, is sure to seize on and to support a "benefactor" who introduces his amendment as a reasonable, practical, but comparatively modest proposal, and then everything goes to hell.

Yes indeed, here in Russia, *le mieux est l'ennemi du mal*! The Gracchi would have been stoned here, at their first steps. One had only to hear what was said today at the meeting by the well known Slavophile, "the old man of the sea" as I call him—long-bearded A. F. Vasilyev—to understand to what absurd lengths things could be taken were we to leave them in the hands of the learned theoreticians of the Slavophile camp. When Vasilyev began to speak of Russia's future western frontiers and started to include Austria inside our future boundaries, both I and many others present literally could not restrain our mirth—even though he tried somehow or other to justify each of our territorial acquisitions historically, geographically, or ethnographically.

"Vasilyev!"[30] I said to him, "the frontiers you are proposing are completely fantastic. We need a map which will please the Russian people, but it must also be acceptable to Europe and acknowledged by our allies. What you propose could only be accepted by the lunatics among them."

He glared at me: "What is Europe to us? Slavs live here and it has been ours since time immemorial." He said, and jabbed at the map with his finger.

After Vasilyev had been speaking for an hour, the chairman managed with some difficulty to stem

105

the fount of his political verbosity and to stop his fantastic Slav reveries, and the meeting returned to a considered discussion of our eastern and western boundaries on the basis of a map drawn up by specialists in the Society's membership.

At 12 midnight, before the meeting ended, I left and returned home.


## 7 December 1916

The sessions of the extraordinary conference of the United Nobility began.

The object was the drafting and presentation of a loyal address to the Sovereign which would point out the grave danger that threatens both the dynasty and Russia as a result of the influence which irresponsible dark forces, i.e., in other words Rasputin and all of his court and official-bureaucratic cliques, exert on all organs of the state apparatus.

The Sovereign just does not see or does not want to see the precipice onto which our homeland is being pushed by his evil genius, Alexandra Fyodorovna.

I listened intently to the speeches of the nobles. The meeting was extremely crowded, for whole provincial delegations which had broken with the Council of the United Nobility in the wake of principled disagreements on political issues, have now returned to the fold. It becomes more and more clear to me that the address will be imbued both with a sense of genuine loyalty and of a proper audacity freed of any possible hint of slavishness or of any effort to conceal the bitter truth.

The speeches of the nobles at the meeting were dignified, imbued as they were with the profoundest grief and oblivious to any personal interest or rank or class. They considered it a moral duty, in these difficult times, to tell the Tsar the plain truth; that truth which is seen and known by the whole Russian people, but which flatterers, hypocrites, and court lackeys dressed in gold-embroidered uniforms hide from the Tsar.

Presiding over the meeting was Prince Kurakin, intelligent, able, and a man suffused with a profound patriotism.

There was hardly a discordant note in the speeches. The usual people, so familiar at ordinary meetings of the United Nobility, had faded into the background, for they regarded the highlight of their activity in the United Nobility as being a dinner at the house of Kontan or Medvyed.[31]

There was no sign of the Astrakhan noble Sergeyev, nor of the noble windbag Pavlov. They had disappeared, faded away. There was no place for them today, for the nobility was not asking anything for itself, it was not speaking of its needs, or of the interests of its class but, as the first estate of the Empire, it was appealing to the Tsar in the name of his people, in an effort to protect the Tsar, as the most sacred possession of the Russian state system.

I have rarely seen greater unanimity than I observed at today's significant and historic gathering.

Count A. A. Bobrinsky,[32] that cautious politician, a refined, intelligent and honest courtier, and the perspicacious V. I. Gurko[33] spoke the same language as the modest gentry who had come from faraway, god-forsaken corners of Russia, and who had brought with them the accumulated feelings of spiritual grief and bitterness.

No, the nobility has not died, no matter how many times it has been buried by the newspaper scribblers of the Kadet camp. Surely the Tsar will heed the voice of his servants who, like faithful subjects, risk approaching him with bitter words of unembellished truth.

The rare voices of protest against the general mood aroused feelings of disgust toward those speakers who, evidently even now, hope to gain something for themselves by playing up to those dark forces against which the nobility, in total unity with the whole Russian people, have taken up arms.

Senator Okhotnikov's speech, which disapproved of the mood of the nobility, was met with profound silence by the assembly, which understood that Okhotnikov spoke not as a loyal and honest servant of the Tsar, but as a slave. I listened as he spoke and remembered this stock market "financier" and the many dark sides of his past activities. I looked with loathing at this clean-shaven physiognomy that lectured the nobility on the concept of duty, honor, and loyal devotion.

V. Gurko spoke superbly, though with notes, and Counts Olsufyev and Musin-Pushkin both spoke sensibly.

During a recess I put my name down, intending to speak on several points in the projected "address" drawn up by a special committee of the United Nobility's Council and provincial representatives. At the end of my speech I had intended to name those individuals who now could honorably hold responsible ministerial posts, but V. Gurko, to whom I had confided my intention, took me by the arm, and in a state of alarm begged me, God save us, not to do this: "You know, don't you, that the results will be just the opposite. The Sovereign will think that we are trying to instruct him, and anyone you name, instead of being brought to power, will be sent immediately to join the ranks of the political corpses, complete with first-class burials. You know that the Tsar cannot bear to be instructed. In God's name, and for the sake of everything, give up this idea."

I agreed with him and, going up to the chairman's desk, crossed my name off the list of speakers.

After the recess, and following a brief debate, a draft of this loyal address was read by Prince Kurakin and, amid thunderous applause lasting at least five minutes, the draft was accepted with very slight alterations by the whole assembly (which voted by districts). Then, the nobles silently began to disperse, conscious of having honestly performed a great patriotic duty.

During the voting on the address, my attention had been drawn to a figure, the moral character of which assumed its full, unprepossessing height before me at this meeting. This was the figure of Myatlev, the Marshal of the Nobility of Novo-Oskolsky in the Kursk district, and a brilliant contemporary poet-pamphleteer.

Who, among those who live in Petrograd and attends fashionable salons and drawing rooms has not in his time copied out for himself one or another of Myatlev's popular poems, all of which treat maliciously and very wittily with Russia's social and political defects, and not even sparing the Tsar?

"What! . . . You haven't read Myatlev's latest poem?" You are usually asked with astonishment by X, Y, or Z, and immediately someone in the salon will take out of his notebook a tattered piece of paper with the poet's latest production, generally of a lampooning nature.

"There you are," they say to you, "copy it out for yourself." And, there and then you copy out the poem which travels anonymously from hand to hand and, in a short time, spreads throughout Petrograd, and almost as quickly to all of Russia.

Myatlev's satire, cutting and spiteful, castigates everything he considers worthy of his attention, sometimes most amusingly, and without sparing the Emperor himself.

I have always found this last fact very irritating, for in my final opinion, the Tsar should not figure in a satirical work, no matter how talented it is, for this damages the prestige of him who must, in the eyes of the people, stand on a high pedestal and whose name cannot be worn out in tomfoolery. This is what I have thought earlier and how I think now.

While all those around me, on reading his work were saying: "How cleverly he writes" or "He has really given it to them, the rascal—what a daredevil," I thought that Myatlev was a blunt and impudent fellow. But today at the meeting of the nobility I saw what that "dare-devil" poet Myatlev really is, in a moral sense. Because of the absence of charming Prince Dundukov-Izyedinov, Myatlev was at the meeting as the head of the Kursk provincial delegation. Feeling that adoption of the address by the Kursk province would make him primarily responsible for the vote because of the position he held by chance, Myatlev strained every effort to get the Kursk nobility to speak against adoption of the address that had been edited by the special committee of the nobles' congress. For, in his, Myatlev's, opinion, the nobility could not speak to the Tsar in such language.

I simply did not believe my ears as I watched him frantically working his nobles, entreating them not to join the other province which were unanimous in support of the address.

"So that is what you are?" I kept repeating to myself in disgust. "You consider it permissible, on the sly, anonymously, to make fun of the Tsar in lampoons, and to bandy his name about. But to raise your voice here, openly, honestly, and directly, together with the nobility does not suit you. Lackey," I thought, he trembles for his chamberlain's uniform and is afraid of losing his chamberlain's key. When? In such times as these!

*9 December 1916*

The most fantastic rumors are circulating again in town about changes in the highest governmental posts. Today I went to the Duma, where a telegram is being passed around, sent, so they say, by Rasputin to the Empress Alexandra Fyodorovna, who is visiting army headquarters. Whether this telegram is apocryphal or whether it really exists, its text is being passed by word of mouth: "While the Duma is thinking and conjecturing, God has decided: the first appointed will be Ivan and the second Stepan." It is being explained thus: Shcheglovitov (Ivan) is marked down by Rasputin for the post of Prime Minister and Beletsky (Stepan) for Minister of Internal Affairs. Whether this is so or not, we shall soon see. Everything is possible for each day brings ever new surprises.

Alexandra Fyodorovna manages Russia as if it were her own boudoir, but people who are appointed to ministerial posts, thanks to her and Rasputin, feel so insecure that they do not even move into the official apartments, but stay in their own.

Our times recall pages from the reign of Pavel Petrovich:[34] No one can be sure of the future and people who are in favor today might find themselves on the streets tomorrow.

. . . . . . . . . .

I am in no condition to view all of this without pain and I ask myself: "Is it possible that the Sovereign is powerless to lock up this woman who is destroying him and Russia in a convent, this evil genius of the Russian people and the Romanov dynasty? Is it possible that the Sovereign does not see where she is pushing us? How she discredits monarchical principles and disgraces herself? Though, as for that, I am sure that her personal relationship with Rasputin is pure and he has only managed to bewitch her on religious grounds." But the things people are saying! "The Tsar is with Yegor,[35] but the Tsarina is with Grigor." —I heard this with my own ears from a group of young soldiers yesterday as I drove along the Zagorodny past the barracks of the Semyonov regiment. It is hard for us monarchists to hear such things. But can one punish these vulgar fellows, these jesters who say out loud what everyone silently and bitterly observes?

My God! Whatever I may be doing, wherever I am, with whomever I may be, whatever I may be talking about, I am nagged by the same thought everywhere and always: As long as this disgrace to

Russia lives, each hour can bring some new surprise, each day he soils the reputation of the Tsar and his family more and more. Already filthy rumours spread among the rabble have affected the Grand Duchesses and the pure and chaste daughters of the Tsar. Yet this reptile, this Khlyst[36] becomes daily stronger, appointing and dismissing high Russian officials and arranging his filthy, mercenary affairs through charlatans like Simanovich[37] and Prince Mikhail Andronnikov.[38]

. . . . . . . . .

All the best and the most honest people who, from time to time, dare to complain against him to the Tsar, are immediately exposed to disfavor and disgrace. There is no administrative post, however lofty, which can protect any great noble who dares to point out to the Tsar how intolerable Rasputin's continued influence on the course of Russian politics and governmental affairs is. Where is A. D. Samarin, the most honest and noble of men who had been Ober-Procurator of the Holy Synod? He was dismissed. He turned out to be unsuitable because he could not reconcile himself to the role of executor of Rasputin's will, nor could he endure having monks like Varnav, Mardary, and Putyat in episcopal posts; so with Rasputin's aid some director of women's courses, one Rayev, was put in his place. Rayev is an ignorant and completely unknown character, as is his assistant in managing the Church's affairs, that feeble-minded Prince Zhevakov, who was appointed in the same fashion.

Where is Prince Vladimir Orlov, the head of the Palace Chancery? He spoke out against Rasputin and had quickly to vacate the Palace.

Where is General V. F. Dzhunkovsky? The same fate befell him despite his closeness to the Tsar.

Where are the maids of honor, the Princesses Orbelioni and Tyutcheva, who for many years were the governesses of the Grand Duchesses? They are not at Court because they dared to raise their voices against Rasputin.

Only those who are protected by that reptile remain in power. And, of course, the highest palace posts are therefore held by that Messalina, [39] Anna Vyrubova, and that knavish swindler, the palace commandant Vladimir Voyeikov.

The Sovereign has fallen completely under the influence of his wife. He regards any mention of Rasputin's pernicious hold over the court by even his most faithful and loyal subjects as interference in his family affairs. My God, how well I understood, when reading Bismarck's memoirs, his hatred of the Empress, Wilhelm I's wife.

Rukhlov, the former Minister of Transport, once told me that one day when, during his report to the Tsar, Rasputin's name cropped up in some connection, the Sovereign immediately stopped listening to him, began to drum his fingers on the table and, turning his face towards the garden, looked intently out the window. Rukhlov understood immediately that further talk on this theme would end badly for him and so, interrupting his remarks on the subject that touched on Rasputin, he turned to another.

Honesty, decency, integrity, selflessness are now worthless, and the only ones who can be found in power are those who, to put the kindest interpretation on it, are able to close their eyes to Rasputin's activities and are ready to carry out unquestioningly his orders, large numbers of which are sent day after day in his monstrously illiterate notes to members of all departments and administrative offices in Petrograd, starting with ministers and ending with petty clerks.

The failure to carry out Rasputin's wishes, expressed in the form of ultimata, instantly calls down on the refractory clerk the revenge of the whip, and the appointment to his post of someone who is obedient, pliable, and incapable of opposing [Rasputin's] will.

The Empress Alexandra Fyodorovna, who looks at everything and everyone through the eyes of Rasputin, divides the employees of all government offices into two groups: "Those who are with us" and "those who are not with us." The first are encouraged by every means and the second are gotten rid of little by little—replaced by "those who are with us."

. . . . . . . . . . . . . . . . .

The other day Prince A. P. Oldenburgsky was relating what he had run into at Headquarters where he had gone with a report to the Sovereign. Having arrived at Mogilev, he would have liked to have been received by the young Empress who, while at Mogilev, was staying on her train at the station, not at the palace with the Emperor.

The Prince could not be received by the Tsarina for, although it was fairly late, she was still sleeping.

On inquiring on why the Empress was resting and whether she was ill, the Prince received the reply that Her Highness was well but that she had been discussing state affairs with A. S. Vyrubova late into the night. Being curious about what precisely had occupied the Empress, the old Prince discovered that Alexandra Fyodorovna and her maid of honor Vyrubova had spent the better part of the night marking plusses and minuses on the directory of ranks of the Petrograd bureaucratic world, dividing them into their supporters and their opponents.[40] Once he had assured himself that what he had been told was indisputable fact, it took the honest and noble Prince a long time to recover from his amazement and his bitterness.

What awaits us tomorrow? That is the question which anyone who is the least bit concerned about the causes of this political abra-cadabra now ruling Russia, has the right to raise. Personally, I can see no ray of light ahead. The Sovereign's will is paralyzed and the result is that there can be no stability in policy. This was made vividly clear to me from one piece of evidence, comparatively minor, but utterly characteristic.

. . . . . . . . . . .

On the third of November when I was reporting to the Sovereign at Mogilev on the situation in the area of Rena, Brailov, and Galatz on the Rumanian front, I dwelt on the activities of Admiral M. M. Veselkin. He had occupied an important military post in this region for nearly two years of war and had become a great expert on our tactical situation there and had displayed exceptional administrative ability and feverish energy in supplying our troops with all necessities. This was extremely valuable since the Rumanians, having allied with us on the very eve of the declaration of war by the Central Powers, and having decided that we would supply them with all the necessary supplies, had sold absolutely everything they possessed in the way of food supplies and military equipment . . . to the Austrians at great profit to themselves. They assumed that they would get everything they needed from us. As a result of these financial deals of theirs, Rumania was as bare as a bone and the Russian army found itself in a desperate situation; a situation further aggravated by a cholera outbreak along the Danube estuary and the terrible state of the Polish-built single track railroad which ran through Russian territory and which was woefully insufficient for meeting wartime needs or for satisfying the most minimal needs of provisioning, military equipment, sanitation, or transport for our desperate armies—living half-clothed, half-shod, and near starvation.

. . . . . . . . . . .

Veselkin worked there without respite day and night, looking into everything, devoid of pedantry, formality, and ignoring red-tape. Tens of thousands of Russian soldiers, arriving there emaciated from hunger, were indebted to him for spiritual and physical support . . . .

An incredible curser and as foul-mouthed as any Russian sailor, but very warm-hearted and sensitive, Veselkin took heroic measures to supply our armies with all the necessities. And the necessities even included the telephone wire to connect our various headquarters, for those Rumanian scoundrels had sold all their wire to their future enemies on the eve of allying with us.

During my stay in Rena, Veselkin had told me that he was preparing to go to Mogilev in order to report to the Sovereign on the disgraceful conditions there, all because of the absence of needed bridges across the Danube and the uselessness of the railroad line (this could be put into proper order quickly if our railway engineers got down to it with a will).

"Unless this is done, we will never achieve anything on this front," Veselkin had added.

The Sovereign Emperor had been at Rena well in advance of my stay there and had seen Veselkin's work. He liked him very much, and that he valued his work was clear from the words of his private telegram to the Empress from Rena, the text of which was passed on to me in Rena by the local Post and Telegraph authorities.

. . . . . . . . . . .

The Sovereign telegraphed to Alexandra Fyodorovna as follows:

"I saw Misha Veselkin. He is rendering inestimable services in this area, etc., etc." This long telegram from the Sovereign to the Tsarina was of a personal nature and was signed Niki or Niks.

And so, on the day of my report to the Sovereign on November 3, when I was describing the situation on this front and touched on the beneficial work of Veselkin, the Sovereign became very animated, was exceedingly pleased with my description of him and, interrupting my report, said: "Oh yes, I have known Veselkin for a long time. He is a fine, able administrator, doing what needs to be done, particularly in the present military situation. I value him highly and set great store by him. I am pleased with your opinion of him."

That was on November third at Mogilev, yet on the seventh of that same November, the following occurred in Petrograd: at eleven o'clock in the morning I entered the State Duma on my way to the Budget Committee which was in session.

As I walked through Catherine Hall, I. K. Grigorovich, the Naval Minister, came toward me. We greeted each other and then he asked me straight away:

"V. M., when did you get back from the front, and from where?" I had hardly had time to open my mouth and say "Today, from the Rumanian front," when Grigorovich, interrupting me, put his arm sympathetically on my shoulder and said bitterly:

"Really? And isn't it a pity about our poor M. M. Veselkin?"

. . . . . . . . . .

"What happened?" I asked.

"Dismissed," said Grigorovich dejectedly.

"That's impossible! Why did you do that?" I exclaimed, "when he is so useful there, so indispensible, and the Sovereign, who knows his work, has a very flattering opinion of him."

Grigorovich smiled bitterly at this. "That is just it, it wasn't I who dismissed him and the Naval Ministry was the last to find out about it. He was dismissed directly from Headquarters yesterday. We don't know through whose machinations or why, but Admiral Nenyukov has already been appointed in his place."

"Listen, Ivan Konstantinovich," I said, "what you are telling me is indeed absurd. You see, the

Sovereign was praising him to me as recently as November third . . ."

"Yes," Grigorovich emphatically noted, "but that was on the third and today is the seventh. You know better than anyone else that here in Russia these days, evaluations of people, especially of those in administrative posts, are not made in reference to the actions of the administrator, but depend on the mood in certain circles."

I sighed, shrugged my shoulders, and we parted.

Is it possible to rely on any "policy" in Russia in the face of such phenomena?

. . . . . . . . . . . .

### 10 December 1916

I heard today that Kaufmann-Turkestansky, the Chief Plenipotentiary of the Red Cross at the Sovereign's Headquarters, has been dismissed from his post. They say that the dismissal was the result of Rasputin's intrigues, for the Empress Alexandra Fyodorovna was extremely perturbed that Kaufmann had not only spoken sympathetically of my speech of the 19th of November to the Sovereign, but had also brought a verbatim report of it for His Highness to read.

### 11 December 1916

Today I went to the Duma to invite its members to inspect my hospital train before it leaves for the Rumanian front. Many of my colleagues, having heard, as they said, good reports on my detachments at the front, had repeatedly asked me to show them how I have organized things.

I invited the members of the Duma to visit the Warsaw Station at nine o'clock on the morning of the 17th of December because I plan to leave for the front that evening.

I purposely chose that date for, if Rasputin has been successfully done away with on the night of the 17th, then nothing could be better than to show my train to a large group of people who are interested in this work just a few hours later, as if nothing had happened. This will also deflect my thoughts from the nightmare of the previous night.

The only question is, will my nerves hold out, and will I have been able to sleep, if only for a few hours, in those hours of the night left to me for sleep after Rasputin's death, and before the members of the Duma visit the train?

But, my train is worth a visit. I look at the results of my troubles in supplying it with pride and satisfaction, and I find it agreeable to think that I will be distributing all of this there, at the front, in a foreign land—to our native heroes, to our soldiers and officers who have stood guard over Russia's honor and have waged uninterrupted war for more than two years, side by side, in close brotherhood, sharing the same privations and living equally in the grim conditions of the trenches.

. . . . . . . . .

*12 December 1916*

Today I was at a meeting of the Chief Administrative Council of the Red Cross. Now here is an institution that is striking for its inertia. There are altogether only two or three people there, among whom are Ordin and Chamansky (a shrewd man who twists the rest around his little finger and plays first fiddle, to his own advantage, of course).

Ilyin, the honorable president, is swaddled up like a baby and occupies a position somewhere between a Buddhist monk and the Dalai Lama. The rest are either supernumeraries in the roles of "wedding-guest generals,"[41] or titled riff-raff who have come to regard figures [and statistics] as the only serious business, and are insensitive to the really great work of mercy.

What is the good of someone like Baron A. F. Maindorf, whose sand clearly has been spilling for some twenty years and yet is nonetheless still in an active position on the Red Cross Council?

I sat there for a half hour and listened to an interminable debate on whether or not to give a forty-ruble allowance to the sisters X, Y, and Z. I was sick of this "practical business" and left.

. . . . . . . . . . . .

*13 December 1916*

This morning the phone rang: "Vanya has arrived." This means that we are to meet.

At ten o'clock I arrived at Yusupov's with Dr. Lazovert.

Dmitri Pavlovich and Lieutenant S. were already there.

Yusupov reported to us that Rasputin had agreed to visit him on the 16th of December and that everything was going superbly. Together we went over the plan we had drawn up again, and decided that once Rasputin was dead, we would throw his corpse into the Old Nevka where, at night, there is a more secluded spot than along the canal running from the Fontanka to the Tsarskoe Selo Station.

In addition to what we had planned earlier, we decided to place a large gramophone in the lobby outside the Prince's drawing room and located above the dining room into which Rasputin would immediately go on his arrival. [The dining room] is, as I have already said, in the cellar of the Palace.

. . . . . . . . .

The gramophone will be placed near the winding staircase with its horn pointed toward it, and when Rasputin arrives at the Palace, the gramophone will be turned on; for although the gramophone is a feeble and tiring distraction, it is nevertheless a distraction. The playing of it will achieve two aims: first, Rasputin might think that a party of ladies was above listening to music and consequently that the young Countess, for whose acquaintance he was so eager, would be unable to come down to him immediately; and second, the sound of the gramophone might drown out our voices, if we had failed to hear the approach of the car and went on talking loudly upstairs.

At eleven o'clock, having eaten and had tea, we were all leaving for our own homes when, just as I was about to go out, Yusupov took a medium-sized, two-pound rubber dumbbell, like those used for indoor gymnastics from his desk.

"How do you like this?" he asked me.

"What do you want that for?"

"For no special reason," he remarked significantly. "Just in case. I got this little present from V. A. Maklakov. You never know what might happen."

"M-mmm, yes," I drawled.

We said goodnight and I left.

. . . . . . . . . . .

*14 December 1916*

In view of our forthcoming departure for the front, I moved my family onto the train today. I am taking my sons along as medical orderlies during their Christmas vacation, and my wife, who has already completed a nursing course and who was senior Sister at one of the advance dressing-stations in my detachment all last summer, will go along to work as a nurse at the supply and dressing-station which I am establishing in Rumania. Their move took a good half of the day.

After lunch I finally bid farewell to my town apartment and moved into my usual compartment in the coach of my hospital train.

. . . . . . . . . . . . . .

*15 December 1916*

Dr. Lazovert, having bought a brush, khaki paint, and dressed in a leather apron, spent all day today on the car which will serve us tomorrow night to fetch our exalted guest.

All the cars in my detachment have inscribed on them, in large red letters, my motto: *Semper idem.*[42] This inscription will have to be painted over, for if by chance there should be some unfortunate turn of events, then this inscription could be that clue that could immediately lead the authorities to the Yusupov Palace and to my train.

By evening the car seemed to be ready. Tomorrow it only remains to put up the top and let the drivers go off to their homes early. The pretext for this will be to give them leave to say goodbye to their families prior to our departure (fixed for the evening of the 17th of December), but in reality, it is to be free of their tiresome curiosity, and their questions about where Dr. Lazovert could be going late at night without needing their services. Already today, as he was tinkering around the car, the train crew, crowding around him, asked just why he was crossing out the inscription. Lazovert lied his way out of it very successfully:

"As soon as we are on the road, chaps," he told them, "we'll have it on again as it was before. But tomorrow night I will be on a spree with . . . (and he winked), and then a drive on the island, and you cannot have a general's car (i.e., my car) being seen at such an hour in such an improper place." The curious ones were satisfied with this and left it at that.

. . . . . . . . . . .

*16 December 1916*

It is now seven o'clock in the evening. I have not gone into the city all day, but have sat reading in my compartment. There is nothing left to do, the train is ready to depart and I could not bear to see any outsiders.

At 8:30 I shall go by tram to a small meeting of the Town Duma where I will stay, in order to kill time, until 11:45. Then, Dr. Lazovert, dressed as a chauffeur, is due to arrive at the Duma watch-tower in an empty car, and once I am seated inside, we will drive on to Yusupov's Palace.

I feel very calm and self-possessed. Just in case, I am taking brass knuckles and my revolver—a splendid object, a *Sauvage*. Who knows, perhaps I will need to use one or the other of them.

I do not know why, but lines from a Horace ode have been running through my head all day long:
*Tu ne quaesieris, scire nefas, quem mihi, quem tibi,*
*Finem di dederint Leukonoe!*[43]
Yes! But that was about something else altogether, and our Leuconoa is of a somewhat different kind . . . indeed! *Scire nefas*! But we haven't long to wait now . . . .

. . . . . . . . .

*18 December 1916*

It is late at night. There is complete silence all around me. My train, rocking easily, speeds off into the distance. I am off again to fresh work, to a military environment so dear to me at a distant outpost in Rumania.

I cannot sleep. The impressions and events of the last forty-eight hours fly around my head like a whirlwind, and the nightmarish, unforgettable night of the 16th of December reappears sharply and vividly in my mind's eye.

Rasputin is no more. He is dead. It has pleased fate that I and no other should deliver the Tsar and Russia of him, that he should fall by my hand. Thank God, I say, thank God that the hand of the Grand-Duke Dmitri Pavlovich was not stained by that filthy blood—he was only a witness and that was all. Even if it was a very patriotic act, a pure, young, and noble, regal youth, so close to the throne, cannot and must not be blamed. For it was, nevertheless, an act which involved the spilling of blood, if only Rasputin's blood.

No matter how difficult it may be, I must try and put my thoughts in order and, with photographic precision, enter in my diary the whole course of the drama that has just occurred and which has such great historical significance.

However difficult it may be, I will try to resurrect the events and put them down on paper.

. . . . . . . . .

At half past nine on the evening of the 16th of December, I left my train at the Warsaw Station and set off by tram for the Town Duma. I arrived there and saw that the hall was not lit up. The porter informed me that the meeting had been cancelled because there had not been a quorum present, and that those who had come, having waited a little, had left.

"Well, old boy," I said, "I have no place else to go. Open up the deputy-mayor's office for me and get me some paper. I will write a few letters here until my car comes for me." The porter carried out my request and I spent about an hour writing letters to a few friends.

At a quarter to eleven, i.e., exactly an hour before I had arranged for Lazovert to come for me at the Duma, I sealed the last letter and found myself undecided about what to do. If I got dressed and went out to the street to wait for the car there, that might prove to be uncomfortable. It could also look suspicious because I was dressed in military uniform, and it might seem strange to see a figure in military garb standing on the sidewalk with nothing to do at eleven o'clock at night.

. . . . . . . . .

I decided to spend the rest of the time on the telephone and, calling a lady-friend of mine, the actress N., I chatted with her until after eleven.

To stay any longer in the Duma, however, would have been awkward, so I put on my coat and went out to the sidewalk. As the clock in the Duma tower struck 11:15, I dropped my letters into a mail box and began to stroll along the side streets near the Duma.

. . . . . . . . . . .

The weather was mild. It was no more than two or three degrees below zero and a light, moist snow was falling.

Each minute seemed like an eternity to me, and I imagined that every passerby looked at me suspiciously and stared after me.

The clock struck half past eleven and then a quarter to twelve. Clearly I did not know what to do with myself. Finally, at ten minutes to twelve, I saw the bright lights of my car in the distance, coming from the direction of Sadovaya. I recognized the characteristic sound of its engine and in a few seconds, Dr. Lazovert turned around and stopped along the curb.

"You're late again!" I shouted at him.

"Sorry," he replied in an ingratiating tone, "I was mending a tire—it burst on the way."

I got into the car next to him and, turning toward the Kazan Cathedral, we drove off along the Moika.

It was absolutely impossible to recognize my car with its top up. It looked no different from the other cars we passed on the road.

. . . . . . . . . . . .

According to the plan we had worked out, we were to have driven not to the main entrance of the Yusupov Palace, but to the small one to which Yusupov intended to bring Rasputin as well. To do so, we had first to enter the courtyard which was separated from the street by an iron grill fence with two pairs of iron gates. According to our agreement these should have been open at this hour.

As we drove up to the Palace, however, we saw that both pairs of gates were closed. Concluding that it was still too early, we maintained our speed and drove on past the Palace. Then, slowing down, we circled around the Mariinsky Theatre Square and returned to the Moika by way of Pracheshny Lane. Again the gates turned out to be closed.

I was beside myself.

"Let's go to the main entrance!" I shouted to Lazovert. "I will go in through the front door and when they open the iron gates, you can drive in and park the car over there by that small entrance."

I rang. A soldier opened the door to me and, without taking off my overcoat, but looking around to see who else was in the foyer (there was one other man dressed in a soldier's uniform sitting on a bench, but no one else), I turned to the door on the left and went into the apartment occupied by young Yusupov.

I entered and saw all three of them sitting in the office.

"Ah!" They exclaimed in unison, "*Vous voilà.* We have been waiting for you for five minutes already. It's after midnight."

"You could have been waiting much longer," I said, "if I had not had the sense to come in the main entrance." And, turning to Yusupov, I said, "The iron gates to your side entrance are still not open."

"Impossible," he exclaimed, "I will see about it right away," and with these words he went out.

I took off my coat. Several minutes later Dr. Lazovert, dressed in his chauffeur's uniform, came in with Yusupov by way of the stairs from the courtyard. The car had been parked at the agreed-upon place— by the small door in the courtyard. Then the five of us went out of the drawing room, through the small lobby and down the spiral staircase to the dining room, where we sat down around a large tea table abundantly spread with cakes and other delights.

. . . . . . . . . . . .

The room was quite unrecognizable. I had seen it before it had been finished and was amazed that it had been possible to turn the cellar into a sort of elegant *bonbonnière*.

It had been divided into two sections: one, nearer a fireplace (in which a fire was blazing brightly and cosily), was a miniature dining room; and the other, in the rear, was something in between a drawing room and a boudoir, with easy chairs, and a low, elegant divan, before which lay an enormous, exceptionally white bearskin. Along the wall, under the windows, a small table stood in semidarkness. On it was a tray with four unopened bottles of marsala, madeira, sherry, and port, and behind these were several smoked wine glasses. On the mantlepiece, among a row of antique pieces, a crucifix of astonishing workmanship had been placed. I think that it had been chiselled from ivory.

The ceiling was vaulted in the style of ancient Russian decorated chambers.

We sat down at the round tea table and Yusupov invited us to drink a glass of tea and to try the cakes before they had been doctored.

The quarter of an hour which we spent at the table seemed to be an eternity to me. There was no need for any special hurry because Rasputin had warned Yusupov earlier that his various spies would not be leaving his apartment until after midnight and if Yusupov were to arrive at Rasputin's before half past twelve, he might run into a Cerberus[44] guarding the "venerable old man."

Once we had finished our tea, we tried to give the table the appearance of having been suddenly left by a large group frightened by the arrival of an unexpected guest. We poured a little tea into each of the cups, left bits of cake and piroshki on the plates, and scattered some crumbs among several of the crumpled table napkins. All of this was necessary so that Rasputin, on entering, would feel that he had frightened a gathering of ladies who had fled the dining room for the drawing room above.

. . . . . . . . . . . .

Once we had given the table the necessary appearance, we got to work on the two plates of petits fours. Yusupov gave Dr. Lazovert several pieces of the potassium cyanide and he put on the gloves which Yusupov had procured and began to grate the poison onto a plate with a knife. Then, picking out all the cakes with pink cream (there were only two varieties, pink and chocolate), he lifted off the top halves and put a good quantity of the poison in each one, and then replaced the tops to make them look right. When the pink cakes were ready, we placed them on the plates with the brown chocolate ones. Then, we cut up two of the pink ones and, making them look as if they had been bitten into, we put these on different plates around the table.

Lazovert then threw the gloves into the fire and we got up from the table, leaving several chairs in disorder as well, and decided to go upstairs. But, just then, I remember it clearly, the chimney began to smoke. Thick smoke filled the room and we had to spend at least another ten minutes in clearing the air. Finally everything was in order.

We went up to the drawing room. Yusupov took two phials of potassium cyanide in solution from his desk and gave one to Dmitri Pavlovich and one to me. Twenty minutes after Yusupov had left to

pick up Rasputin we were to pour these into two of
the four glasses sitting behind the bottles on the
table in the dining room below.

. . . . . . . . .

Lazovert dressed himself in his chauffeur's outfit,
Yusupov put on his overcoat, raised his collar, and
saying goodbye to us, left.

The noise of the car told us that they had gone
and we silently began to pace up and down in the
drawing room and in the lobby by the stairs which led
below.

It was twenty-five minutes to one. Lieutenant S.
went to see if the gramophone worked and if a record
was on it. Everything was ready.

I took my heavy *Sauvage* from my pocket, which
had been weighed down by it, and placed it on
Yusupov's table.

Time passed painfully slowly. We did not feel
like talking. We exchanged occasional words only—
asking should we smoke, or would the smoke of a
cigar or a cigarette drift downstairs (Rasputin did not
want Yusupov to have any male guests on the night
of his visit), and then we began to smoke earnestly, I
my cigar, and S. and Dmitri Pavlovich their cigarettes.

. . . . . . . . . . . .

At a quarter to one the Grand-Duke and I went
down to the dining room and poured the potassium
cyanide into two of the wine glasses, as we had agreed
to do. At this point Dmitri Pavlovich expressed his
fear that Felix Yusupov might, when offering cakes
to Rasputin, eat a pink one in his haste or, when

pouring out the wine, take one of the poisoned glasses by mistake.

"That will not happen," I assured the Grand-Duke firmly, "as I see it, Yusupov is remarkable for his great composure and his presence of mind."

Once we had finished this task, we went back upstairs, where we strained to hear the slightest sound from the street.

"They are coming," I suddenly said in a half-whisper, moving away from the window.

Lieutenant S. rushed to the gramophone and in a few seconds we heard the sound of the American march "Yankee Doodle," a tune which haunts me even now.

· · · · · · · · ·

An instant later we heard the dull rumble of the car already in the courtyard, and then the slamming of the car door, the stamping of feet shaking off the snow, and the voice of Rasputin saying: "Which way, my dear?"

Then the dining room door closed behind both arrivals and after a few minutes Dr. Lazovert came up the stairs to us wearing his usual clothes—he had taken off his chauffeur's fur coat, Astrakhan hat, and gloves, and had left them below.

Holding our breath, we went down the lobby and stood near the banister of the stairs leading below. We stood bunched together: I was first on the staircase, the brass knuckles in my hand; behind me was the Grand-Duke; behind him Lieutenant S.; and last was Dr. Lazovert. It is difficult for me to determine how long we stood tensely waiting in these fixed poses by the staircase, trying neither to breathe nor move, but listening intently to literally every rustle that came from below. The voices of the speakers did reach us—sometimes as monosyllabic sounds, sometimes as snatches of conversation—but we were unable to understand what they were saying. I suppose we must have stood there on the staircase for at least half an hour, constantly rewinding the gramophone which continued to play the same old tune, "Yankee Doodle."

. . . . . . . . . . . .

What we were expecting did not happen. We were expecting to hear the popping of corks and Yusupov opening the bottles which, as I have already said, were arranged downstairs. This would have told us that things were going well and that in a few more minutes Rasputin would be a corpse. But . . . time passed. The quiet conversation continued down below and the speakers, evidently, were still not eating or drinking anything.

At last we heard the door below opening. On tiptoes we rushed noiselessly back to Yusupov's study where, a minute later, he entered.

"Just imagine, gentlemen," he said, "nothing is going right. The beast will neither eat nor drink. No matter how much I urge him to warm up and accept my hospitality."

What can we do?

Dmitri Pavlovich shrugged his shoulders: "Have patience, Felix, go back and try again, and do not leave him by himself, not for a minute. He could come up here after you and see something he had not expected, and then we would either have to let him go in peace or else finish him off noisily—this could be fraught with consequences."

"What sort of mood is he in?" I asked Yusupov.

"N-not very good," drawled the latter, "you can just imagine, he seems to have some sort of premonition."

"Well, go, go, Felix!" The Grand-Duke began to hurry Yusupov out, "time is slipping away."

Yusupov again went downstairs and we took up the same positions as before by the staircase.

. . . . . . . . . . .

Another good half-hour had passed by agonizingly for us before we clearly heard the popping of two corks, one after the other, the tinkle of glasses, and then the sound of voices speaking suddenly fell silent.

"They are drinking," Dmitri Pavlovich whispered in my ear. "Well, now we won't have long to wait!"

We went down several steps further on the staircase and then froze in our positions. But . . . another quarter of an hour passed while the quiet conversation and even the odd laugh went on and on down below.

"I do not understand this," I whispered, turning to the Grand-Duke and throwing up my hands. "Can he be so enchanted that even potassium cyanide won't work on him?"

Dmitri Pavlovich just shrugged.

"Just a minute, listen, there... I think that there is something amiss down there."

And, indeed there did seem to be a groaning sound. But, it turned out to be a trick in our hearing, because a minute later the peaceful manner of

conversation from one of the speakers and mono-
syllables, apparently from the other, was again audible
from below.

. . . . . . . . . . .

We all filed back up the stairs and went into the
study. After two or three minutes Yusupov entered
noiselessly. He was distraught and pale.

"No," he said, "it is impossible. Just imagine, he
drank two glasses filled with poison, ate several pink
cakes and, as you can see, nothing has happened,
absolutely nothing, and that was at least fifteen
minutes ago! I cannot think what we can do, especially
because he has already begun to worry about why the
Countess is taking so long to come to him. I had
difficulty in explaining to him that it is hard for her
to disappear unnoticed, for there are not many
guests up here, and that probably she would be down
in about ten minutes. He is now sitting gloomily on
the divan and the only effect that I can see of the
poison is that he is constantly belching and that he
dribbles a bit."

"Gentlemen, what do you advise that I do?"
Yusupov implored.

"Go back," we said. "The poison is bound to
take effect finally, but if it nevertheless turns out to
be useless, come back here after five minutes and we
will decide how to finish him off. Time is running
out. It is already very late and the morning could find
us here with Rasputin's corpse in your Palace."

Yusupov walked slowly out of the room and
went downstairs.

. . . . . . . . .

Just then I noticed that Dr. Lazovert was not with us. A little earlier I had noticed that this powerfully-built man was getting positively ill with agitation. Now he would pace nervously around the study, beet red from apoplexy, and then he would sink exhausted into the deep armchair under the window, hold his head and cast a roving look at all of us.

"What is the matter with you, doctor?" I had asked him.

"I am ill," he answered me in a half-whisper. "My nerves are exceedingly strained. I do not think that I can stand it. I never thought that I had so little self-control. Believe me, a five-year-old could knock me over right now."

I was very surprised. During the whole time that Dr. Lazovert had been with my detachment, he had shown himself to be a man of great endurance, self-possession, and undoubted courage. He had worked repeatedly in forward positions and had not only been under artillery fire, but had also faced enemy machine gun fire, for which he had twice been awarded the George Cross.

"Yes," I reflected, "bravery is one thing there, but here it is quite a different matter."

"Where is Lazovert?" I asked Lieutenant S. after Yusupov had left.

"I do not know," replied the latter. "He must be with the car."

"That is strange," I thought, and was about to go down after him when I saw him coming in the study door, pale and haggard.

. . . . . . . . . . . .

"Doctor, what is the matter with you?" I cried.

"I started to feel ill," he whispered, "I went down to the car and fainted. Fortunately I fell face down, the snow cooled my head and only thanks to that did I come to. I am ashamed, V. M., I am absolutely good for nothing."

"Doctor, doctor," Dmitri Pavlovich said, walking past us and shaking his head, "don't say such a thing!"

"Your Highness," Lazovert answered, throwing up his hands in a gesture of apology, "I cannot help it, it's my constitution."

We left Lazovert in peace, leaving him to himself, and went back to waiting.

. . . . . . . . . . . .

About five minutes later Yusupov appeared in the study for the third time.

"Gentlemen," he rattled out at a fast pace, "the situation is still the same. The poison is either not acting on him or else it is no damn good. Time is running out, we cannot wait any longer. Let's decide what to do. But we must decide quickly, for the reptile is showing extreme impatience because the Countess has not come, and he is getting very suspicious of me."

Ah well," replied the Grand-Duke, "let's forget it for today, let him go in peace. Perhaps we will be able to send him packing some other way another time and in different circumstances."

"Never!" I exclaimed. "Your Highness, don't you understand that if he gets away today, he will have slipped away forever. Do you think that he will come to Yusupov's tomorrow once he realizes that

139

he was tricked? Rasputin cannot," I continued in a half-whisper, stressing each word, "must not, and will not leave here alive."

"What is it to be, then?" asked Dmitri Pavlovich.

"If poison doesn't work," I answered, "then we must show our hand. Either we must all go downstairs together, or you can leave it to me alone. I will lay him out, either with my *Sauvage* or I'll smash his skull in with the brass knuckles. What do you say to that?"

"Yes," said Yusupov. "If you put it like that, then of course we will have to settle for one of those two methods."

After a brief conference, we decided that we would all go downstairs and that I would lay him out with the brass knuckles. But, just in case, Yusupov slipped his rubber dumbbell into Lazovert's hands, though the latter assured him that he would hardly be in a position to do anything because he was so weak that he could hardly walk.

This decision taken, we started carefully toward the staircase, walking in single file (with me at the head). We were already on the fifth stair when Dmitri Pavlovich suddenly tapped me on the shoulder and whispered in my ear: "*Attendez un moment.*" Then he climbed back up the stairs and took Yusupov aside. Lazovert, S., and I returned to the study where we were soon joined by Dmitri Pavlovich and Yusupov. The latter said to me:

. . . . . . . . .

"V. M., will you object if, come what may, I shoot him? It will be quicker and simpler."

"Not at all," I replied. "It is not a question of who kills him, but that he be killed, and without fail, tonight."

I had barely pronounced these words before Yusupov, with a quick, resolute stride, went to his desk and, removing his small Browning from a drawer, turned quickly and went purposefully down the stairs.

We silently rushed out after him and resumed our old positions, knowing that now there really would not be long to wait.

. . . . . . . . .

Indeed, five minutes had not passed since Yusupov's departure when, after hearing two or three scraps of conversation from below, there came the dull sound of a shot, and then we heard a prolonged A-a-a-a!, and the sound of a body falling heavily on the floor.

Without delaying a second, those of us who had been waiting upstairs literally flew, head over heels, down the banisters and smashed into the dining room door. It opened, but one of us got caught on the light switch, which immediately cut off the electricity in the room.

. . . . . . . . .

Groping our way along the wall by the door, we switched on the light and were met by the following scene: in front of the divan, in the lounge area of the room, Grigory Rasputin lay dying on the white bearskin, and standing over him, holding a revolver behind his back in his right hand, was Yusupov, perfectly calm, gazing with an expression of indescribable disgust at the face of the "venerable old man" he had killed.

There was no blood visible. Evidently it was an internal hemorrhage—the bullet had entered Rasputin's chest and had not come out.

The Grand-Duke was the first to speak, and turning to me, said: "We must get him off the rug quickly, just in case, and put him on the tiled part of the floor. His blood might ooze out and stain the bearskin. Come on, let's get him off there."

Dmitri Pavlovich took the dead man by the shoulders, I lifted him by the feet, and we placed him carefully on the floor with his feet toward the window facing the street and his head toward the staircase from which we had come.

There was not a drop of blood on the rug; it had only been a little flattened by the falling body.

． ． ． ． ． ． ． ． ． ． ． ．

We stood silently around the body of the dead man, whom I was seeing now for the first time in my life, and whom I had hitherto only known from photographs. One of which, a large one, depicting him at a tea-table surrounded by a circle of his admirers from the Petrograd court aristocracy, had been given to me by the commander of the third guards regiment, General A. P. Usov. I had had a large number of copies made of this and, together with an insulting inscription for his admirers, whose names I had added to the cards, I had distributed them at the end of November to members of the State Duma and had sent copies to the editors of all the Petrograd newspapers.

Now as I was standing over this corpse, I was seized by the most diverse and profound feelings. The first of them, as I now recall, was one of the profoundest astonishment that such a commonplace, repulsive looking Silenus[45] or satyr, this peasant, could have had such influence on the fate of Russia, and on the way of life of a great people whose country represents not just a government, but a large part of the globe.

. . . . . . . . . . . .

"You scoundrel, how did you bewitch both the Tsar and the Tsarina?" I thought.

"How did you get such a hold on the Tsar that your will became his will, that you were the actual autocrat of Russia, and turned the anointed of God into an obedient, unquestioning executor of your malevolent wishes and your rapacious appetites. Standing there over this corpse, I involuntarily recalled Yusupov's story of how Rasputin had treated the Tsar with something he had obtained from his friend, the Tibetan medicine man Badmayev.[46]

Rasputin had once said to Yusupov, "Felix, why don't you go and visit Badmayev, he is indispensible and very useful. Go see him, my dear, he has some wonderful herbal remedies—he uses only herbs. If he gives you just a very tiny little glassful of one of his herbal concoctions—oo!. . .! You get such a longing for wenches! He has another mixture which, if he should give you an even smaller glassful of that and you drink it when you are feeling troubled, all your problems will dissolve and you will become such a nice, decent fellow, so silly and innocent, and nothing will seem to matter to you anymore."

· · · · · · · · ·

Standing over Rasputin's corpse, I wondered whether this wasn't the extract which he had lately been giving to the Russian Tsar as he relinquished the reins of government over mighty Russia and over his people to that "wicked witch,"[47] that woman so fatal to Russia, his wife Alexandra Fyodorovna, who thought herself a second Catherine the Great, and compared you, Sovereign, to Peter III. In her letter to the Grand-Duchess Victoria Fyodorovna she wrote shamelessly that there are times in the history of peoples when, because of the weak will of their rulers, women take over the reins of government— justified by the weakness of the male—and that Russia knows of such examples.[48]

· · · · · · · · · · ·

I stood over Rasputin watching him intently. He was not yet dead. He was breathing, in agony.

He had covered both his eyes and half of his long spongy nose with his right hand. His left arm was stretched along his body; and, every now and then, his chest rose high and his body twitched convulsively. He was smartly dressed, not at all like a peasant: magnificent boots, velvet trousers worn outside the boots, a cream shirt richly embroidered in silk and belted by a thick, crimson silk cord with tassels.

His long black beard had been painstakingly combed and seemed to shine, or glistened from some sort of hair-oil.

I do not know how long I stood there. Finally, Yusupov's voice rang out: "Well, gentlemen, let's go upstairs, we have to finish what we have begun." We left the dining room, turning out the light and leaving the door slightly ajar.

In the drawing room, we each congratulated Yusupov, on whom the great honor of freeing Russia of Rasputin had fallen, and then hurried to finish our work.

. . . . . . . . .

It was already after three o'clock in the morning and we had to hurry.

Lieutenant S. hastily put on Rasputin's smart fur coat over his military uniform, slipped on his high overshoes, and held his [Rasputin's] gloves in his hand. Then, Lazovert, who had recovered a little and seemed to have calmed down, put on his chauffeur's clothes and, led by the Grand-Duke Dmitri Pavlovich, they all left for the station and my train to burn Rasputin's clothes in my passenger coach, where by then the stove should have been hot. When they had finished with this, they were to take a cab to the Grand-Duke's Palace and then come back to Yusupov's Palace in his car for Rasputin's body.

Felix Yusupov and I were left together, but not for long. He went through the lobby to his parents' apartments—they, apparently, were not in Petrograd at that time. While waiting the return of our accomplices, with whom we proposed to bind up the corpse in some cloth and drag it to the Grand-Duke's car, I began to smoke my cigar and to pace slowly around his study.

. . . . . . . . . . . .

145

I can't say whether I was alone for long. I only know that I was feeling quite calm and even satisfied. But, I do remember clearly how some inner force pushed me toward Yusupov's desk where my *Sauvage*, which I had taken from my pocket, lay; how I picked it up and put it back in the right hand pocket of my trousers; and how, under the pressure of that same mysterious force, I left the study, whose hall door had been closed, and found myself in the corridor for no particular purpose.

I had hardly entered the hallway when I heard footsteps below near the staircase, then the sound of the door—which opened into the dining room where Rasputin lay—which the person entering evidently had not closed.

· · · · · · · · ·

"Whoever could that be?" I wondered, but before I had time to give an answer, a wild, inhuman cry, which seemed to come from Yusupov, suddenly rang out: "Purishkevich, shoot! Shoot! He's alive! He's escaping!"

"A-a-a-a! ..." and the figure which came rushing headlong, screaming up the stairs, turned out to be Yusupov. He was as white as a sheet and his fine, big blue eyes were even larger than usual and bulged out of their sockets. He was insensate and almost oblivious to my presence, and with a mad look he rushed through the door which led to the main lobby and ran through to his parents' apartments (to which I had seen him go, as I have already said, after the Grand-Duke and Lieutenant S. had left for the station).

I was dumbfounded for a second, but then I began to hear quite clearly from below someone's rapid, heavy footsteps making their way to the door leading to the courtyard, i.e., to that entrance from which the car had recently left.

There was not a moment to lose so, without losing my head, I pulled my *Sauvage* from my pocket, set it at *feu*, and ran down the stairs.

. . . . . . . . .

What I saw downstairs could have been a dream, had it not been so terribly real. Grigory Rasputin, whom I had contemplated half an hour earlier, taking his last gasp heaving from side to side on the stone floor of the dining room, was now running swiftly on the powdery snow in the courtyard of the Palace and along the iron-railed fence which led to the street, dressed in the same clothes in which I had just seen him lifeless.

. . . . . . . . . . .

At first I could not believe my eyes, but his loud cry, breaking the silence of the night, as he ran: "Felix, Felix, I will tell the Tsarina everything . . ." convinced me that it was he, that it was Grigory Rasputin, and that he might, given his phenomenal vitality, get away. In just a few more seconds he would be through the double iron gates and on the street where, without identifying himself, he could ask the first chance passerby to save him, because his life was being threatened in this Palace. Then . . . all would be lost. Naturally they would help him, not knowing who it was they were saving, and he would find himself back home on Gorokhovaya, and we would be exposed.

. . . . . . . . . . .

I rushed after him and fired.

In the dead silence of the night, the incredibly loud noise of my revolver shattered the air—missed!

Rasputin ran faster. I fired a second time as I ran and . . . . missed again!

I cannot express how enraged I was with myself at that moment.

I was a better than average shot; I regularly practiced shooting small targets on the firing range at the Semyonovsky parade-ground, but today I was not able to lay out a man at twenty paces.

. . . . . . . . . . .

Seconds passed. . . Rasputin had already reached the gates when I stopped, bit my left hand as hard as I could to make myself concentrate, and with one shot (the third one), hit him in the back. He stopped and this time, taking careful aim from the same spot, I fired for the fourth time. I apparently hit him in the head, for he keeled over face first in the snow, his head twitching. I ran up to him and kicked him in the temple with all my might. He lay there, his arms stretched far out in front of him, clawing at the snow as if he were trying to crawl forward on his belly. But he could no longer move and only gnashed and gritted his teeth.

. . . . . . . . . . .

I was convinced that now his song had really ended and that he would not get up again. Standing over him for several minutes, I satisfied myself that there was no point in guarding him any longer. I then walked quickly back to that same little door and into the Palace. I remembered clearly that in the intervals between my shots at Rasputin two men had come along the sidewalk on the street. The second of them, on hearing a shot, had rushed away from the fence and run off.

"What is to be done? What is to be done?" I kept saying out loud as I went into the drawing room. I am alone, Yusupov is out of his mind, and the servants don't know what is going on. The corpse is lying there by the gates and at any moment could be noticed by a chance passerby. Then there would be hell to pay. I couldn't drag him by myself, and even the idea of touching Grigory Rasputin filled me with loathing and disgust. But, there was no time to lose.

"No," I decided, "since things have not gone as we had planned from the very beginning, they must now take their course." Perhaps the servants had not heard Yusupov's shots in this room, but it was impossible to imagine that two soldiers sitting in the main entrance hall could not have heard four loud shots from my *Sauvage* in the courtyard. I walked through the lobby to the main entrance.

"Boys," I addressed them, "I killed . . . ." At these words they advanced on me in real earnest as if they wanted to seize me. "I killed," I repeated, "Grishka Rasputin, the enemy of Russia and the Tsar." At these last words, one of the soldiers became greatly agitated and rushed up to kiss me. The other said: "Thank God, about time!"

. . . . . . . . . . .

"Friends!" I declared, "Prince Felix Felixovich and I rely on your absolute silence. You understand that if this business is discovered, the Tsarina will not commend us for it. Can you keep quiet?"

"Your Excellency," they both addressed me reproachfully, "we are Russians, you need not worry, we won't betray you."

I embraced and kissed them both, and then asked them to drag Rasputin's body away from the fence in the courtyard immediately, and to put it by the stairs in the small entrance hall leading into the dining room.

This seen to, and having learned where Yusupov had gone, I went to calm him down. I found him in the brightly-lit bathroom. He was leaning over the basin, holding his head with both hands, spitting repeatedly in disgust.

"My dear, what is the matter with you? Calm down, he is already done for! I finished him off! Come with me, my dear, into your study." Feeling obviously sick, Yusupov looked at me glassy-eyed, but he obeyed. Putting my arm around his waist, I led him gingerly into his apartment.

As he walked, he kept repeating: "Felix, Felix, Felix, Felix . . . ." Evidently, something had passed between him and Rasputin in that brief moment when he had gone down to the dining room to what he had thought was a corpse. Whatever it was, it had impressed itself strongly on his brain.[49]

We walked through the lobby just as Yusupov's soldiers were dragging the corpse into the entrance hall at the bottom of the stairs.

. . . . . . . . . . . .

Seeing what they were doing, Yusupov broke away from me and ran into his study where he grabbed the rubber dumbbell that Maklakov had given him from his desk and returning, flung himself downstairs to Rasputin's corpse. Having poisoned him and seen that the poison didn't work, having shot him and seen that the bullet hadn't killed him, he evidently could not believe that Rasputin was already dead. He ran up to him and began to beat him on the temple with the two-pound rubber weight with all his might, in a sort of frenzy of quite unnatural excitement.

As I stood upstairs by the banister, I did not immediately understand what was happening, and then I was even more dumbfounded when Rasputin, to my great astonishment, seemed to be showing signs of life!

He wheezed, and with his face turned upward, I could see quite clearly from above how the pupil of his open right eye rolled as if looking at me senselessly —but horribly (I can still see this eye before me even now).

. . . . . . . . . . .

I soon recovered and shouted to the soldiers to quickly pull Yusupov away from the dead man. If he got himself and everything around him spattered with blood then, if the investigating authorities carried out a search— even without police dogs— the traces of blood would give everything away.

The soldiers obeyed, but it cost them an extraordinary effort to restrain Yusupov who, as if mechanically, but with ever increasing frenzy, continued to hit Rasputin in the temple.

At last they pulled the Prince away. Both soldiers carried him upstairs in their arms and, all covered in blood as he was, rashly sat him down in a soft leather couch in his study.

It was terrible to look at him, so horrible did he look inside and out—with his rolling gaze, his twitching face, and his senseless repetition of "Felix, Felix, Felix, Felix . . . ."

. . . . . . . . . . . .

I ordered the soldiers to hurry and find some cloth from somewhere and to wrap the corpse tightly from head to foot and then to bind the swaddled thing securely with cord.

One of them set off to carry out my orders, but I called the other upstairs a few minutes later and, having heard from him that the policeman on duty at the corner of Pracheshny and Maximilian lanes, had come to find out what the shooting had been about, and that when he went off duty in half an hour he would have to report what had happened in his district to his superior, I told him to bring this policeman to me.

. . . . . . . . . . . . . . . . . .

Ten minutes later the soldier led the policeman into the study. I quickly looked him over from head to foot and at once realized that I had made a mistake in calling him in; he was a veteran of the old school. Nevertheless, I had to deal with things as they were.

"Officer," I addressed him, "Did you come here a little while ago to inquire about what had happened and why there had been a shooting?"

"That is right, Your Excellency." he replied.

"Do you know me?"

"That is right," he replied again, "I do."

"Who am I then?"

"State Duma member Vladimir Mitrofanovich Purishkevich!"

"Right!" I said. "But do you know this gentleman?" I pointed to Yusupov who was still sitting in the same position.

"I do," replied the policeman.

"Who is he?"

"His Highness, Prince Yusupov!"

"Right! Listen, brother," I continued, putting my arm around his shoulder, "answer me honestly: Do you love our holy Tsar and Mother Russia? Do you want the victory of Russian arms over the Germans?"

"Of course, Your Excellency," he replied. "I love the Tsar and the fatherland and I want victory for Russian arms."

"And do you," I went on, "know who is the most evil enemy of the Tsar and of Russia, who hinders our war effort, who puts Shturmers and all sorts of Germans in the Government, and who controls the Tsarina and, through her, makes short work of Russia?"

The policeman's face brightened immediately.

"Yes," he said, "I know, Grishka Rasputin!"

"Well, old boy, he is no more. We killed him—it was him we were shooting at just now. You heard, but if anyone asks you, you can say: 'I saw nothing and I know nothing.' Can you manage to be quiet and not betray us?"

. . . . . . . . . . .

The policeman became thoughtful. "It's like this, Your Excellency, if they ask me, and I am not under oath, then I will say nothing, but if they put me under oath, then it can't be helped, I will have to tell the whole truth. It would be a sin to lie."

I realized that talking would lead nowhere and, learning that his duty was up in half an hour and that his district chief was Lieutenant Grigoryev (who was, as far as I knew, a very decent fellow of good family), I let him go in peace, deciding to leave the future to fate.

. . . . . . . . .

The soldier came in and reported that the corpse was already wrapped up.

I went down to have a look. The body was tightly wrapped in some sort of blue material (it even seemed to me to be a window curtain) and was bound securely with cord. The head was covered. Now I could see that Rasputin was undoubtedly a corpse and that he could not come to life again.

There was nothing more to do but to wait patiently for the return of the Grand-Duke, Lazovert, and Lieutenant S. So, for the last time I went up to Yusupov's study and, after handing him into the care of his servants, and asking them to hurry and help him clean up, and change his clothes and shoes, I sat down in an armchair and began to wait.

About five minutes later there came the sound of a car and then the Grand-Duke and his companions came quickly up the stairs from the courtyard and into the study.

Dmitri Pavlovich was in an almost cheerful mood, but when he looked at me he knew that something had happened.

. . . . . . . . . . .

Looking around, he asked me what had happened.

I quickly explained the situation to the newcomers and asked them to hurry, but this last request was unnecessary. They understood that there was not a moment to be lost and so, leaving Yusupov in the care of one of his soldiers, we dragged Rasputin's corpse into the Grand-Duke's car together with the chains and the two 2-pood weights I had brought to Yusupov's apartment that night. We all got into the car and drove off to the place we had chosen for interring the dead man's corpse.

This time the driver was the Grand-Duke, with Lieutenant S. sitting next to him. Dr. Lazovert sat in the back on the right, I sat on the left, and, squeezed in with the corpse, was the second of Yusupov's soldiers, whom we had decided to take with us to help us throw the heavy body into the hole in the ice.

. . . . . . . . .

We were already on our way when I noticed that Rasputin's overshoes and coat were in the back of the car. "Why weren't these burned on the train as we agreed?" I asked Dr. Lazovert. "Now you have brought them all back!"

"It is because," he replied, "the coat, naturally enough, would not go into the stove in one piece, and your wife decided that it was impossible to start ripping and cutting it up in order to burn it in pieces."

155

"She even had a row with Dmitri Pavlovich over them and so we were forced to bring back the coat and the overshoes. We did burn his sleeveless coat, his gloves, and I don't remember what else."

"Well, we will have to throw the coat and the overshoes into the water with the corpse," I said.

"And, gentlemen, did you telephone to the Villa Rodé as we had agreed?" I inquired further.

"Yes, of course," he replied, "it has been done."

We fell silent and continued the journey thus.

The car travelled fairly slowly through the city. It was very late and the Grand-Duke evidently feared that great speed would attract the suspicions of the police.

The windows of the car were open. The fresh, frosty air had an invigorating effect on me. I was quite calm, despite all that I had been through. But, one after another, thoughts of Rasputin and his past, of all the efforts (even by members of the Imperial family), to rid the Tsar of this reptile, clear and distinct thoughts and images of the struggle against Rasputin, rushed, like a whirlwind in my head.

. . . . . . . . . . . .

I remembered my visit to the Grand-Duke Nikolai Mikhailovich at the beginning of November, immediately after my return from the front—a visit once again linked with the name of Rasputin. I recalled how Glinsky, the editor of *The Historical Herald*, had telephoned me to pass on an invitation from the Grand-Duke Nikolai Mikhailovich, asking me to come see him whenever it was convenient for me. I remembered how I struggled with myself over whether or not to go. I really did not like the Grand-

Duke Nikolai Mikhailovich's historical works because in them he presented his royal forefathers in the most unattractive fashion, sullying their names.

However, I decided to set a date for the visit, and went to see him.

. . . . . . . . .

I was met in the study by a decrepit old lion wearing the epaulettes of an adjutant-general and who, for some reason, spoke with an eastern accent. His very first words dwelt on the dreadful situation in which Russia and the Romanov dynasty had been put, thanks to Rasputin's exclusive influence on the Tsar and Alexandra Fyodorovna.

I was astonished by the candor of the Grand-Duke, whom I had only just met, on coming to see him. But, evidently, he was seething with too much resentment and he wanted to test himself and his mood against the mood of other Russians whose views and goals were different from his own. (I found out later from Yusupov, who had lunched with him on that day, that two hours after my visit, he had had a visit from Burtsev.)[50]

He spoke almost the whole time without pausing, occasionally looking at me questioningly, to which I replied with an approving nod or a brief "yes," "true," or "of course."

"You know, V. M.," said the Grand-Duke, "that almost the whole of our Romanov family submitted the Sovereign a memorandum on Rasputin, asking him to take the reins of the Russian state into his own hands and to put a stop to the interference in governmental affairs by the Empress Alexandra Fyodorovna, who is wholly inspired by that Khlyst. As should have been expected, of course, nothing came of this memorandum. I did not even sign it, for I saw that it was useless and I knew that a memorandum, and especially one on this subject, would change nothing, but would have deplorable results for those who had signed it.

. . . . . . . . .

"I did something else," the Grand-Duke Nikolai Mikhailovich said. "Having received an important assignment from the Sovereign, in carrying it out, I wrote a report which went straight to the crux of the matter. In this report I indicated clearly, vividly, but as if incidentally, the full horror of the contemporary social mood of Russia, a mood with which I am very familiar and which is the result of the Rasputinite control over Russia and of the pervasive interference of the Tsar's wife, who is alien to the people and to Russia.

"Once I had completed the report," continued the Grand-Duke, "I asked the Sovereign, when he was in Petrograd, to name a day so that I could deliver it to him orally. I added, however, that 'I fear that after my report you will have me arrested and exiled far from the capital with the Cossacks.' "

" 'Is your report so dreadful?' the Sovereign asked, naming the day. 'Well, what can we do, we will hear you out and hope that it all turns out peacefully.' So I gave him my report, and the result: I am in disgrace, out of favor, and treated with complete coolness. If you like," said the Grand-Duke as he finished his story, "I'll read you this report." I expressed a desire to hear it and Nikolai Mikhailovich read me a short but forceful and sharply worded memorandum, in which the attention of the Sovereign was drawn to the fact that, in the event of further interference by Alexandra Fyodorovna and Rasputin in state affairs, the dynasty would be threatened with ruin and the Russian Empire with catastrophe.[51]

. . . . . . . . . . .

I recalled that when the Grand-Duke had finished reading the memorandum, I sat, impressed by what I had just heard, as if hypnotized for several minutes. I only came to when the Grand-Duke offered me a cigar and added: "You know, I sent this report through Prince Shervashidze to the Empress Marya Fyodorovna in Kiev. Would you like to know the opinion of the Dowager Empress? Here it is." And, rummaging through some papers, the Grand-Duke handed me a telegram to read. There were only three words on it: "Brave, bravo, bravo, — Marya." "But, cautious Shervashidze," added the Grand-Duke, "was evidently afraid to leave such a compromising document as my memorandum among the old Tsarina's papers so, look (here Nikolai Mikhailovich handed me a letter from Shervashidze), he returned my memorandum which had provoked so much sympathy and approval from the Dowager Empress together with this letter to me expressing the apprehension that I might be without a document that I need . . . ."

These were my recollections as I sat in the rear of the car, with the lifeless corpse of the "venerable old man," which we were taking to its eternal resting place, lying at my feet.

. . . . . . . . . . .

I looked out the window. To judge by the surrounding houses and the endless fences, we had already left the city. There were very few lights. The road deteriorated and we hit bumps and holes which made the body lying at our feet bounce around (despite the soldier sitting on it). I felt a nervous tremor run through me at each bump as my knees touched the repulsive, soft corpse which, despite the cold, had not yet completely stiffened.

At last the bridge from which we were to fling Rasputin's body into the hole in the ice appeared in the distance.

Dmitri Pavlovich slowed down, drove onto the left side of the bridge, and stopped by the guard rail.

The bright headlights of the car flashed for an instant across a sentry box on the other side of the bridge to the right, but when the Grand-Duke turned off the lights, it was plunged into darkness. The car engine continued to clatter in neutral.

. . . . . . . . . . .

I opened the car doors quietly and, as quickly as possible, jumped out and went over to the railing. The soldier and Dr. Lazovert followed me and then Lieutenant S., who had been sitting by the Grand-Duke, joined us and together we swung Rasputin's corpse and flung it forcefully into the ice hole just by the bridge. (Dmitri Pavlovich stood guard in front of the car). Since we had forgotten to fasten the weights on the corpse with a chain, we hastily threw these, one after another, after it. Likewise, we stuffed the chains into the dead man's coat and threw it into the same hole. Next, Dr. Lazovert searched in the dark car and found one of Rasputin's boots, which he also flung off the bridge.

All of this took no more than two or three minutes. Then Dr. Lazovert, Lieutenant S. and the soldier got into the back of the car, and I got in next to Dmitri Pavlovich. We turned on the headlights again and crossed the bridge.

. . . . . . . . .

How we failed to be noticed on the bridge is still amazing to me to this day. For, as we passed the sentry-box, we noticed a guard next to it. But, he was sleeping so deeply that he had apparently not even waked up when, on our arrival at the bridge with the corpse, we had inadvertently lit up not only his sentry-box, but had even turned the lights on him.

. . . . . . . . . . .

Once we had crossed the bridge the Grand-Duke increased his speed, but there was something wrong with his car. The engine kept misfiring and we had to stop several times because the car refused to run.

Each time this happened, Dr. Lazovert jumped out, fiddled with the spark plugs, cleaned them, and somehow or other got us going again.

The last stop and repair occurred on Kameno-Ostrovsky Avenue, nearly opposite the Petropavlovsk fortress. After cleaning [the plugs] there, we went faster, and arrived successfully at the palace of Sergei Alexandrovich where Dmitri Pavlovich was staying.

. . . . . . . . .

On the way back, I had told the Grand-Duke about what had happened at Yusupov's Palace while he had been away burning the dead man's clothes. Having finished my story, I said to him: "You know, Dmitri Pavlovich, I think that our big mistake was in throwing the corpse into the water instead of leaving it somewhere conspicuous. It is possible that a false Rasputin might appear, since this craft is a rather profitable one."

"Maybe you are right," the Grand-Duke replied, "but what is done cannot be undone."

Just as we arrived at the palace gates and were getting out of the car, we saw, to our great amazement, Rasputin's second boot, which we had overlooked. At the same time, we saw spots of blood which had trickled from the dead man onto the carpet of the car.

The Grand-Duke instructed his servant, who had met us on the steps and who struck me as having been initiated into the whole affair, to burn the carpeting and Rasputin's boot. Then, Lieutenant S., Dr. Lazovert, and I said goodnight to Dmitri Pavlovich. From the palace we took two cabs to the Warsaw Station: Lieutenant S. to pick up his wife who had spent the night with mine, and Dr. Lazovert and I to sleep for the few hours which remained before the Duma delegation arrived at 9 o'clock to inspect my train.

. . . . . . . . . . .

It was already after five in the morning when, having paid the cabby on the bridge of the Warsaw

Station, we made our way to my coach. Nobody noticed us; everyone slept like the dead.

In the corridor of the coach we caught sight of the white nurse's kerchief belonging to my wife. She had waited for us to return. Then each of us crept quietly into his compartment. I fell asleep immediately without undressing.

· · · · · · · · ·

It was before half past eight on the morning of the 17th of December when, who would have thought it given the night we had spent, Dr. Lazovert and I, fresh and invigorated, prepared to receive our Duma guests. We had already posted medical orderlies by the coaches when they appeared at about nine o'clock with A. I. Shingarev, as the doctor at their head.[52] An elaborate examination of the train went on until almost midday as we gave them every possible bit of information on the work of our detachment.

Soon after twelve o'clock the members of the Duma left and I, seated in my car, drove off to say goodbye to my mother, and then drove on to the State Duma to send a telegram to V. Maklakov in Moscow: "When are you arriving?" signifying, as had been stipulated, that Rasputin was dead.

From the State Duma I drove to Prince Oldenburgsky's palace to see General Kochergin, the head of his chancery, and finally, after three, I drove to Engineer Street to the Red Cross headquarters to meet with its director, Chamansky.

· · · · · · · · · · ·

All of these visits, for which I found some pretext (my train was already fully equipped), I made with the single goal of insuring that today, from early morning, I would be seen at my usual business, by all sorts of people from every profession and class of society, who could, if the need arose, testify that I was the same today as they have always known me to be.

Shortly after four o'clock I returned to my train, loaded up my second car, and gave instructions to my staff to arrange with the administration for our departure no later than five o'clock. I had hardly sat down to dine with the personnel of my detachment when I heard a car arrive. Lieutenant S. got out and came up to me.

We went to my compartment where S. relayed Dmitri Pavlovich's request that I come to his palace at once.

I got into his car with him and we drove off.

. . . . . . . . . . .

At the palace I found both my host and Yusupov. They were both extremely agitated, and were drinking cup after cup of black coffee with brandy. They declared that they had not slept at all last night, and could not have had a more disturbing day, for the Empress Alexandra Fyodorovna had already been informed of the disappearance and even the death of Rasputin and had named us as his murderers.

. . . . . . . .

The maid-of-honor Golovina, Rasputin's secretary, had provided the information about Grigory

Yefimovich's destination that evening, and all the police and detective departments had already begun their search for the dead man's corpse and to find all of the threads of this affair.

"Because of this reptile," Yusupov remarked, "I had to shoot one of my best dogs and lay him on the spot where the snow was stained with the blood of this 'old man.' "

. . . . . . . . .

"I did this in case our Sherlock Holmeses, lighting on the real tracks of the vanished Rasputin, might want to analyze the blood, or in case they bring in police-dogs. The rest of the night," he concluded, "I and my soldiers spent in putting the house in order, and now, as you can see, V. M., Dmitri Pavlovich and I are composing a letter to Alexandra Fyodorovna, which we hope to get to her this very day."

I helped draft the rest of the letter, which we finished about an hour and a half after my arrival.

When the letter was finished and sealed, Dmitri Pavlovich left the study to mail it to its addressee. All three of us felt rather awkward with each other, for the letter was full of invented lies, and depicted us in the role of unjustly outraged virtue.

. . . . . . . . .

Taking advantage of [Dmitri Pavlovich's] absence, I asked Yusupov, "Prince, tell me, what happened between you and Rasputin in those few minutes when you went downstairs for the last time to the dining room from which we had all exited, you remember, leaving him, apparently, at his last gasp on that cold floor?"

Yusupov smiled sickly, "I won't forget what happened there for my whole life," he replied. "When I went down to the dining room I found Rasputin in the same place. I took his hand to feel his pulse—it seemed to me that there was none—then, I put my palm on his heart—it wasn't beating. Suddenly, you can imagine my horror, he opened wide one of his satanic eyes and then the other and fixed me with a look of indescribable intensity and hatred, and with the words 'Felix! Felix! Felix!' he leapt up to grab me. I jumped away as fast as I could, but remember nothing after that."

*At the Front*

At that moment the Grand-Duke Dmitri Pavlovich returned and, after embracing him, Yusupov, and Lieutenant S., I said farewell and drove back in the Grand-Duke's car to my train. At ten o'clock that evening I left for the front, forsaking the Russian capital, which Dmitri Pavlovich planned to leave the next day, as did Yusupov, who was preparing to join his wife in the Crimea, at Koreiz.[53]

Such was the entire course of events which occurred from the evening of the 16th of December to the evening of the 17th of December.

.......................................................................................

.......................................................................................

.......................................................................................

.......................................................................................

. . . . . . . . . . . .

Day is breaking. I add these lines at the first light of a dawning winter's day.

It is still dark, but I feel that the day is already near. I cannot sleep. A succession of rapidly changing thoughts is rushing through my fevered brain like a whirlwind. I cannot forget myself. I am thinking of the future. Not my petty, personal fate, no, but the fate of that great land which is dearer to me than family or life—that land which I call my homeland.

My God! How gloomy the future is in these difficult years of martial strife sent down to us by the hand of the Almighty.

Will we be able to sustain the whole weight of the burden of these spiritual storms, or will we weaken and, tired and worn out and having lost faith in ourselves, will we also forfeit that place in the world which we have occupied for the many centuries of our historic existence?

Who will say? Who will answer? Who will remove the veil, lift the fog which obscures the distant future?

Are we a great people capable of making our way forward in the channel of our national river, absorbing other tribes and minorities in our waters, or? Or, is everything over for us? Have we become atavisms, ground down by the destructive course of time? Are we doomed to become only an arena for the struggle of other races, other peoples, who will regard the Slavs as an inferior race, fit only for fertilizing the fields of others? Who will tramp their bones, walking toward the light, toward knowledge and world domination, which it is not our fate to achieve?

Who will say? Who will answer? Who can
foretell the flow of events through the thick, milky
mist of the awakening day?

18th December 1916

En route.

## Translator's Notes

1. Tsarina Alexandra Fyodorovna (1872-1918), granddaughter of Queen
   Victoria, daughter of Alice and Ludwig IV, Grand-Duke of Hesse.
2. Mogilev, The Headquarters of the General Staff. Nicholas' decision
   to take personal command of the army and to station himself at
   Mogilev in 1915 is credited by many as having had fatal consequences
   for the Autocracy.
3. B. V. Shturmer (1848-1917). Chairman of the Council of Ministers,
   Minister of Foreign Affairs to 1916. Suspected of pro-German
   sympathies, he was removed and tried for treason in 1916.
4. G. G. Zamyslovsky and N. E. Markov were both members of the
   Pravye, the extreme right of the Duma.
5. A. D. Protopopov (1866-1918), member of the Octobrist Party,
   Vice-President of the Duma from 1914. In 1916 he was appointed
   Minister of Interior. His close association with Rasputin caused a
   public outcry against him.
6. V. N. Voyeikov, Major-General. Palace Commandant.
7. Count A. S. Sheremetev, a member of the Black Hundreds which
   organized pogroms against the Jewish population.
8. V. V. Sabler, Procurator of the Holy Synod, one of Rasputin's
   supporters.
9. N. P. Rayev, Attorney-General of the Holy Synod.
10. N. A. Dobrovolsky, Rasputin's second private secretary, and Minister
    of Justice October 1916-February 1917.
11. Irina Alexandrovna, a niece of the Tsar. Yusupov and his wife shared
    apartments in one wing of his father's palace.
12. Tarpeian rock, a rock near Capitoline Hill in Rome onto which
    traitors were hurled.

13. V. A. Maklakov, Right-wing Cadet, member of the second, third, and fourth Dumas. Minister of Interior in 1913, Ambassador to France for the Provisional Government, 1917. See Maklakov's reply to the publisher of the original Russian version, *supra*.
14. Rasputin's apartments were at No. 64 Gorokhovaya Street.
15. Pravye, the extreme, nationalist right party in the Duma. The majority of its members were drawn from the landowning class of the Southwest provinces.
16. Tsar Ivan III, the Great. The "Gatherer of the Russian Lands," reigned 1462-1505. The original Russian reads: "At a time when Russia should be viewed from the bell-tower of Ivan Velikii . . . ." [the highest tower in the Kremlin.—MES]
17. An obvious anti-Semitic slur.
18. A. I. Guchkov, leader of the Octobrist Party.
19. M. V. Rodzianko, President of the Fourth Duma.
20. This no doubt refers to the pressure these three, among others, will apply to the Tsar in February 1917 to obtain his abdication. If this is a diary, one could credit Purishkevich with a palpable prescience.
21. Cognac.
22. Golovina and her daughter Munya were Rasputin's ardent admirers and had introduced Yusupov to Rasputin. In the Russian version Golovina is called "fraulein" which translates as "lady in waiting." Fraulein is retained here because its use also suggests pro-German tendencies or sympathies. Purishkevich believed Rasputin and the entire court to be guilty of such feelings. [MES]
23. *Istoricheskii vestnik* [*Historical Herald*), a semi-scholarly, monthly historical journal. It was founded by A. S. Suvorin.
24. Count Karl V. Nesselrode, Minister of Foreign Affairs 1816-1856. Baltic German.
25. Prince A. M. Gorchakov, Minister of Foreign Affairs 1856-1882. Gorchakov was well-known for the excellence of his French.
26. Bilibin, a witty character in *War and Peace*.
27. Egeria, a nymph who, according to Roman legend, advised King Numa on religious matters.
28. A. N. Khvostov, formerly a provincial governor. He became Minister of Interior in 1915. A favorite of Rasputin's, he would later be implicated in a plot to assassinate him and be dismissed.
29. The original Russian gives *Ovi* and *arces*. [Translator's note]
30. In the Russian edition the name given is Afanasyi Vasil'evich, an obvious error [translator].
31. Medvyed [bear],a popular nickname for M. V. Rodzianko.
32. A. A. Bobrinsky, Minister of Agriculture from July to November, 1916.
33. V. I. Gurko, formerly P. A. Stolypin's assistant, a nonparty member of the State Council.

34. Tsar Pavel Petrovich, Paul I, reigned 1796 to 1801. Killed in a Palace coup by disaffected nobles, he was succeeded by his son Alexander I.
35. Yegor, slang for the Cross of Saint George.
36. Khlyst, a member of a religious sect of Old Believers. This sect was known for its emotional, even frenzied rituals, and orgies. Many maintain that Rasputin's doctine of salvation through sin originated in his contacts with this sect.
37. A. S. Simanovich, a former diamond-cutter and Rasputin's first secretary.
38. Prince M. M. Andronnikov, personal friend of Rasputin's and Nicholas', the Russian capital's foremost "fixer."
39. Messalina, the third wife of the Emperor Claudius. The name is synonomous with plotting, intrigue, and evil. Anna Vyrubova was the Tsarina's confidante and a close friend of Rasputin's.
40. The "directory of ranks" refers to the Table of Ranks, instituted by Peter the Great. There were fourteen ranks, of which the highest six conferred hereditary status to their holder.
41. "Wedding-guest generals," retired generals who were paid to appear in uniform at weddings or parades.
42. *Semper wem*, in the original. [Translator]
43. "Do not seek to discover Leuconoa, it is not given to us to know what end has been prepared for you or for me by the gods!"
44. A three-headed dog which guards the infernal regions.
45. Foster father of Bacchus, leader of the satyrs.
46. Peter Alexandrovich Badmayev, a Siberian Asian who, after an orthodox medical education, abandoned it for the practice of Tibetan folk medicine. He was a successful practitioner of this art in the Russian capital, treating many prominent members of the aristocracy. It was rumored that he had treated both the Tsarevich and, as Purishkevich would have it, the Tsar.
47. *Zmeya Gorinych* in the original, a witch-woman in Russian folk tales.
48. This was a charge which had become common currency in the Russian capital. Rasputin, too, is said to have compared Alexandra to Catherine, while describing Nicholas as a "child of God." See Yusupov, *Le fin de Raspoutine* (Paris, 1927), p. 125.
49. According to Yusupov, he had checked on the body, and had even shaken it, when he noticed that the face and one eye were twitching. Then, to his surprise, Rasputin jumped up, seized him by the epaulettes, and then fell again. *La fin de Raspoutine*, p. 175.
50. V. L. Burtsev was one of the leaders of the Socialist Revolutionary Party. He founded a counter-intelligence agency which succeeded in unmasking numerous police spies within the revolutionary movement, including Malinovsky. During World War I he supported

the Triple Entente and returned to Russia to offer his services to his long-time foe, the Autocracy.

51. The Grand-Duke, who was the Tsar's cousin, delivered this report to him at Mogilev on the 14th of November. See Pares, *The Fall of the Russian Monarchy*, pp. 389-390.

52. A. I. Shingarev, a member of the Kadet Executive Committee, and after the February Revolution, Minister of Finance in the Provisional Government. Why Purishkevich called him "doctor" is unclear since Shingarev was a professor of constitutional law, not a medical doctor.

53. Despite Alexandra Fyodorovna's efforts, Purishkevich (already under suspicion in Rasputin's disappearance) was allowed to leave for the front. The Grand-Duke Dmitri Pavlovich and Prince Yusupov did not, however, leave Petrograd the next day. They were placed under house arrest by order of the Empress and ultimately, Yusupov was exiled to his country estate and Dmitri Pavlovich was exiled to Persia to serve with the Russian forces there.

# Selected Bibliography

Adams, A. E. (ed.) *Imperial Russia after 1861: Peaceful Modernization or Revolution?* Boston, 1965.

Avrekh, A. *Stolypin i Tret'ia Duma.* Moscow, 1968.

Avrich, P. *The Russian Anarchists.* Princeton, 1967.

Black, C. E. (ed.) *The Transformation of Russian Society: Aspects of Social Change Since 1861.* Cambridge, Mass., 1960.

Charques, R. *The Twilight of Imperial Russia.* London, 1974.

Cherniavsky, M. (ed.) *Prologue to Revolution.* Englewood Cliffs, NJ, 1967.

Chmielewski, E. *The Polish Question and the Russian State Duma.* Knoxville, 1970.

Cohen, S. F. *Bukharin and the Bolshevik Revolution.* NY, 1973.

Curtiss, J. S. *Church and State in Russia, 1900-1917.* NY, 1940.

—————, (ed.) *Essays in Russian and Soviet History.* Leiden, 1963.

de Jonge, A. *The Life and Times of Grigorii Rasputin.* NY, 1982.

Deutscher, I. *The Prophet Armed.* Oxford, England, 1954.

Diakin, V. S. *Russkaia burzhuaziia i tsarizm v gody pervoi mirovoi voiny.* Leningrad, 1967.

Dresler, A. *Rasputin.* Munich, 1929.

Edelman, R. *Gentry Politics on the Eve of the Russian Revolution.* New Brunswick, 1980.

Enden, M. de, *Rasputin et le crépuscule de la monarchie en Russie.* Paris, 1976.

Fischer, G. *Russian Liberalism from Gentry to Intelligentsia.* Cambridge, Mass., 1958.

Florinsky, M. *The End of the Russian Empire.* NY, 1961.

Fulöp Muller, R. *Rasputin, The Holy Devil.* NY, 1928.

Gelai, S. *The Liberal Movement in Russia 1900-1905.* London, 1973.

Gershchenkron, A. "Agrarian Politics and Industrialization: Russia 1861-1917," *The Cambridge Economic History of Europe.* Cambridge, 1966. Vol. VI, pt. II, pp. 706-800.

Getzler, I. *Martov. A Political Biography of a Russian Social Democrat.* Melbourne, 1967.

Golder, F. A. (ed.) *Documents in Russian History.* 1914-1917. NY, 1927.

Gurko, V. I. *Features and Figures of the Past.* Stanford, 1939.

Haimson, L. "The Problem of Social Stability in Urban Russia, 1905-1917," Slavic Review, XXIII (December, 1964), pp. 619-642, and XXIV (March, 1965), pp. 1-22.

—————(ed.) *The Politics of Rural Russia, 1905-1914.* Bloomington, IN, 1979.

Harcave, S. *First Blood. The Russian Revolution of 1905.* NY, 1964.

Healy, A. E. *The Russian Autocracy in Crisis, 1905-1907.* Hamden, Conn., 1976.

Hosking, G. *The Russian Constitutional Experiment: Government and Duma 1907-1914*. NY, 1973.

Judas, E. *Rasputin. Neither Devil nor Saint*. Los Angeles, 1942.

Katkov, G. *Russia 1917. The February Revolution*. NY, 1967.

Keep, J. L. *The Rise of Social Democracy in Russia*. Oxford, England, 1963.

Kerensky, A. *Russia and History's Turning Point*. NY, 1965.

Kochan, L. *Russia in Revolution, 1890-1918*. London, 1966.

Kokovtsov, V. N. *Out of My Past*. H. Fisher (ed.). Stanford, 1935.

Krivoshein, K. A. *A. K. Krivoshein (1857-1921). Ego znachenie v istorii Rossii nachala XX veka*. Paris, 1973.

Kryzhanovskii, S. E. *Vospominaniia*. Berlin, 1938.

Levin, A. *The Second Duma*. New Haven, 1940.

————. *The Third Duma*. Hamden, Conn., 1973.

Liubosh, S. *Russkii fashist, Vladimir Purishkevich*. Leningrad, 1925.

Maire, G. *Raspoutine*. Paris, 1966.

Massey, R. K. *Nicholas and Alexandra*. NY, 1967.

Mehlinger, H. and Thompson, J. M. *Count Witte and the Tsarist Government in the 1905 Revolution*. Bloomington, IN, 1972.

Meyer, A. G. *Leninism*. Cambridge, Mass., 1957.

Miller, M. S. *The Economic Development of Russia 1904-1914*. NY, 1967.

Mosolov, A. *At the Court of the Last Tsar*. E. W. Dickes (tr.). London, 1935.

Oberlander, E. et al. *Russia Enters the Twentieth Century, 1894-1917*. NY, 1971.

Oldenbourg, S. S. *Nicholas II: His Reign and His Russia*. 4 vol., vol 1 ed. and tr. by L. Michalap and P. Rollins. Gulf Breeze, Fla., 1975.

Owen, L. *The Russian Peasant Movement 1906-1917*. NY, 1963.

*Padenie tsarskogo rezhima*. 6 vols. Leningrad, 1924-1927.

Pares, B. *The Fall of the Russian Monarchy*. NY, 1939.

———— (ed.) *The Letters of the Tsaritsa to the Tsar 1914-1916*. London, 1923.

Pearson, R. *The Russian Moderates and the Crisis of Tsarism, 1914-1917*. London, 1977.

Pinchuk, B.-C. *The Octobrists in the Third Duma, 1907-1912*. Seattle, 1974.

Pipes, R. (ed.) *Revolutionary Russia*. Cambridge, Mass., 1968.

———— (ed.) *The Russian Intelligentsia*. NY, 1961.

Purishkevich, V. M. *Iz dnevnika V. M. Purishkevicha: Ubiistvo Rasputina*. Paris, 1924.

Rasputin, M. *My Father*. NY, 1934.

———— and Patte Barham. *Rasputin: The Man Behind the Myth*. NY, 1977.

Robinson, G. T. *Rural Russia Under the Old Regime*. NY, 1932.

Rodzianko, M. V. *The Reign of Rasputin*. NY, 1927.

Rogger, H. "Was There a Russian Fascism?—The Union of Russian People," *Journal of Modern History*. XXXVI (December, 1964), pp. 398-415.

Sablinsky, W. *The Road to Bloody Sunday.* Princeton, NJ, 1976.

Schwartz, S. M. *The Russian Revolution of 1905.* Tr. G. Vakar. Chicago and London, 1967.

Simmons, E. J. (ed.) *Continuity and Change in Russian and Soviet Thought.* Cambridge, Mass., 1955.

Smith, C. J. *The Russian Struggle for Power, 1914-1917.* NY, 1956.

Stavrou, T. S. (ed.) *Russia Under the Last Tsar.* Minneapolis, 1969.

Timberlake, C. (ed.) *Essays on Russian Liberalism.* Univ. of Missouri Pr., 1969.

Treadgold, D., *Lenin and His Rivals.* Westport, Conn., 1955.

Trufanov S. [Iliador] *The Mad Monk of Russia.* NY, 1918.

Ulam, A. *The Bolsheviks.* NY, 1965.

Von Laue, T. *Why Lenin? Why Stalin?* Philadelphia, 1964.

Weidlé, W. *Russia: Absent and Present.* Tr. A. Smith. NY, 1953.

Wildman, A. *The Making of a Workers' Revolution.* Chicago and London, 1967.

Wilson, E. *To The Finland Station.* NY, 1940.

Wolfe, B. *Three Who Made a Revolution.* NY, 1948.

Yusupov, F. *La fin de Rasputin.* Paris, 1927.

—————. *Lost Splendor.* NY, 1953.

Zagorsky, S. O. *State Control of Industry in Russia During the War.* New Haven, 1928.